My Memories

Melvina L. Aaberg

Two Rooms Press / San Francisco

Dedicated to the memory of my dear husband Ted, who had a much better way with words than I, and without whose love many of these memories would never have been. And to my wonderful children and grandchildren—my "crown jewels"—who lovingly enrich my life and bring me more happiness than I can ever put into words.

~ contents ~

~ acknowledgements ~

Writing a book such as this is something I never dreamed would happen when I started entering things into what I called "My Journal" back in August of 2000. For years not much went into it, but then I realized it would be important for my children to know more about my family and my childhood. As life went on the Journal grew to include important events in the lives of my husband, children and myself, and these make up a big part of my memories. I want to thank all of my children for so willingly supplying information I requested and allowing me to quote from their school papers and other writings that I came upon. Marie deserves special thanks for spending hours and hours proofreading and sitting by me at my computer while I made the corrections. My son Ted has spent a great amount of time over the years researching my family history with me through photos, stories, and field trips to Tracy and Garvin, Minnesota. This book would never have been completed were it not for Jonathan, the man of many talents, and making books is one of them. I do not have the words to thank him.
I have been so blessed!

Chapter One

~ Early Years ~

ॐ

August 20, 2000

A beginning of the history of
Melvina Lorraine Olson

I decided to begin this writing today on my 74th birthday at an age I hardly want to admit, but it is so. I was born on August 20, 1926, on my parents' homestead near the small village of Garvin in Lyon County, Minnesota. I was happy to find a beautiful little booklet which my parents had received from the Farmers State Bank, Garvin, Minnesota. On the outside was a picture of a stork carrying a baby in a blanket. Underneath the picture it read, *"Congratulations."* This provided many details about my birth which aren't necessary to include here; however, I did learn some things that surprised me. The nurse on duty was Rena Galstad, who later became my aunt when she married my mother's brother Carl Johnson.

The physician was Dr. Valentine, a fine country doctor, who was still practicing medicine at the time I was married.

The Olson family: Edward, Gerhard
Melvina, Orlando, Marvin
Leonard, Jennie

The following is copied from my Certificate of Baptism:

Melvina Lorraine

Child of Mr. E. G. Olson and his wife Jennie Amalia Olson

Born August 20th, 1926, in Lyon County, Minnesota, was baptized in Höland N.E.L. Church (Norwegian Evangelical Lutheran) on the 19th of September 1926 in the Name of the Father, and of the Son, and of the Holy Ghost.

Pastor U. L. Larsen

Witnesses: Mr. and Mrs. O. C. Olson

Emma Johnson (my mother's younger sister)

Melvin Johnson (my mother's brother)

Now I will begin to write about what I first remember since I, of course, did not remember my baptism but it was the most important first act of which I was a part, outside of being born.

Edward (on right) & brother-in-law John Johnson

Since my father, Edward Gabriel, (1881-1928) died when I was only 16 months old I do not remember anything of him. I know he must have been quite an enterprising young man since he had the foresight to begin purchasing another farm near the homestead we lived on. This was probably since four sons were born before I was born: Gerhard, Marvin, Orlando, and Leonard. This must have been quite a venture since it was also the beginning of the Depression Era.

My Aunt Elma told me once that my dad was her favorite brother and that he was the first in the community to buy a car. No doubt he was pretty proud giving people in the community rides. From pictures that I have I know he was a handsome man, very tall and lean. He must have been a very hard worker which is a trait that has been handed down from generation to generation. I wish I had had the foresight to ask more about my mother and father but it was never talked about. I believe it was because of the sadness surrounding the situation of my parents' dying so young and people just didn't want to talk about it, and I probably didn't want to be reminded about it. Nevertheless, I should have broached the subject and found out many things that I would love to know today. What I do know I learned mostly from write-ups in the <u>Tracy Headlight Herald.</u> My Aunt Elma kept clippings in her scrapbook from the weekly paper where much valuable information was recorded. This has gotten to be one of my most valuable resources.

I understand my father was loading up pigs to take to town and when my mother got uneasy after not hearing from him for a while, she looked out the window and found him lying on the ground. The paper said he died of a ruptured stomach which probably meant a ruptured appendix. He was taken to his heavenly home on January 13, 1928. Gerhard was only 13 at the time our father died and the others all went down in ages from there to me. I was only 16 months old at the time. I am sure of that because I have a photo of myself taken on the front porch of our home which states that I was 16 months old and that it was taken the day after my father's funeral.

Melvina at 16 months

My mother probably became sick with breast cancer even before I was born. I believe she doctored in Tracy for a while with Dr. Valentine and when the seriousness of her sickness was discovered she rode the train by herself down to the Mayo Clinic in Rochester and was a patient at Saint Marys Hospital where she underwent surgery and received radiation treatment. I remember seeing a letter that was written by my father to my mother which said, *"Marvin would like to have gotten on the train with you."* How sad it was that she had to ride the train all alone to Rochester but that is how it was in those days. Someone had to stay at home with the children and do the farm work.

Jennie

I don't remember much about my mother. I do remember having an earache one time and she came with a hot water bottle to soothe the ache. My Aunt Marie (Mother's older sister) was down helping out a lot. As time went on and my mother's health continued to fail it was necessary to get a hired girl to do the cooking and cleaning.[1] In those days being a hired girl was about the only occupation available to a young girl. Many never had the opportunity to attend high school, so they worked at the only thing they knew, housework. I especially remember one time when my mother was quite sick lying in the back bedroom and Dr. Valentine was called. When he came I wanted so badly to go into the bedroom but the hired girl wouldn't let me, so I sat in the windowsill in the kitchen. Probably that was best.

1   Over a period of years there were several girls or ladies hired to help. I remember a couple of them who were hired later on and they will be identified by name as they appear.

The next thing I remember is the night before she died (her bed was in the parlor at that time) and all of us five children knelt down by her bed and said the Lord's Prayer together.

I am sure Olaf and Marie were there also or we probably would not have thought of doing that by ourselves. But how nice that we did. Then in those days the body was prepared for embalming right in the home so she was kept right there and placed in a casket, of course. I just sort of remember ladies with black dresses and hats walking around and I suppose I was kind of milling around amongst them. Of course the funeral was held in Höland Lutheran Church only a

Melvina, Leonard, Orlando, Marvin, Jennie, & Gerhard

short way east up the hill. My grandfather Gunnerius Olson who died in 1903 had donated the land for the church and cemetery. My mother was taken to her heavenly home on November 15, 1930. I understand Rev. U. L. Larsen had a very good funeral sermon - something he was good at. Following are the ages of my family when my mother died: Gerhard 16, Marvin 12, Orlando 10, Leonard 8, and Melvina 4. In June of 2000 Jonathan, Teddy and I took a trip to Tracy and visited the graves of our many ancestors who are buried in the Höland Cemetery.

Shortly after my mother's funeral my uncle Clarence (Mother's brother) had the task of moving me and all my belongings, which probably weren't too many, up to Olaf and Marie's since Uncle Olaf[2] was now my guardian as well

2   I will often be referring to Olaf as Uncle Olaf or Uncle and

as the guardian of my four older brothers. Thank goodness that could be worked out and we didn't just become wards of the state. (It is so important to make provisions for your children in a Will even though you are young and expect to live for a long time.) We all needed a lot of care and supervision not only for our daily needs like food and clothing but the added burden of trying to hang on to the home place and the new farm which my father had been in the process of purchasing. As mentioned earlier Uncle Olaf became our guardian and the sole manager of all the affairs connected with providing for the care of the household with four very young boys as well as for the management of the two farms. If I remember correctly my Uncle Emil, who was my father's half-brother, had loaned him some money earlier which I am quite sure was forgiven. The Stock Market crashed on October 24, 1929, which brought on the Great Depression so those were tough times.

I came across a letter dated January 11, 1931, written by Olaf C. Olson (our uncle and guardian) to Clarence Hanson who later became a hired man down on the farm. His mother also came as housekeeper for my brothers.)

My Dear Mr. Hanson,

Received your letter of the 7th and in answer will say that we have got a lady to come and keep house here now - received a letter from Rev. Gullerud last Saturday saying she was coming in 2 weeks. So we must take her. But

Marie as Aunt Marie or Auntie out of respect for them since they really took over as my parents. It was my home from the age of 4 until I was married.

*she only comes on trial – she says if she does not
like it she wants to be free to quit any time. So
if she should not want to stay maybe we could
manage to get you folks in some way. If you
were to be had at that time. Hoping to see you
soon.*

I remain yours very truly,
Olaf C. Olson

Re: the above letter I can see why the lady would be a
little apprehensive – after all taking care of 4 boys ages 8 to
16. But money was hard to come by and a job is a job.

The three couples are from left to right:
Olaf & Marie Olson,
Edward & Jennie Olson, John & Elma Johnson

Hired Girls: It must have been hard for Uncle Olaf to
oversee the business of hiring girls to do the housework
down at the farm. I only remember three of the very early
ones – the one who wouldn't let me go in to see my moth-

er when the doctor came, another one who let me sit by her on the back steps while she polished her fingernails as she waited for her boyfriend to pick her up, and then there was Mrs. Hanson, the old lady who sent out a black rag to stop the blood from running on Marvin's leg when he got a rock spun into it from the wheel of the old car he was working on.

However there was one I remember very well and that was Mary Moore. She was the housekeeper for several years. I used to go down to the farm in the summertime and stay for several days at a time. I slept with her on the big

Melvina & her brothers
Orlando, Gerhard, Marvin
Melvina, Leonard

double bed in the back bedroom. I was able to help her with some chores around the house. I don't think I was any good at helping with the cooking at that time. She was a good cook and took care of that. I have a picture of her bringing lunch out to the men in the field who were threshing. Bringing out coffee and cake in the afternoons was a must and she was faithful at doing that. Of course I always got to go along. Aunt Marie would also come down and help her when threshing days came around. Mary Moore was the last hired girl they had until the boys took over the cooking and whatever else they could do themselves. They probably got pretty good at it, the cooking anyway.

Brothers: While this story is mostly about my life I do not want to go without writing a little about my brothers.[3] Those were tough days for them on the farm. Uncle Olaf and Aunt Marie spent a lot of time there I am sure. It was remarkable that they were able to keep the farm where they lived as well as the second farm which my father was in the process of buying. Those farms are still in the Olson family today. Gerhard moved to the farm up the hill when he and Bernetta got married. Their children Roberta and Eugene (Buzzy) were raised there. Orlando and Leonard farmed the home place.

Gerhard loved horses and loved going to rodeos. He was a member of the Plum Creek Saddle Club. Marvin probably got pretty good at cooking when they were bachelors. He probably first took to woodworking while he was in Mr. Gray's shop class at Tracy High School. He built a nice vanity for me as one of his projects. More is writ-

---

3   My four brothers attended a small country school, District 72, a mile or so from the farm. I remember their teacher's name, Gladys Herd. She was a dedicated teacher highly respected in the community.

ten about Marvin in another section and his settling in California.

When Orlando got out of the service after World War II he attended classes which were offered by the G I Bill of Rights to acquaint veterans with new ideas about farming, etc. He loved to roller skate and was an excellent bowler. Teddy has a memorial for Orlando on the wall in our basement which displays some of his handiwork. There is a copy of one of his High Score Bowling Cards in that display. Orlando would have been proud that Teddy did this for him.

Melvina & Leonard

Leonard, being the youngest, probably had it the toughest. He lived on the home place his entire life and farmed and also was married and raised his family there. Later he worked for a company doing roadwork and drove some heavy equipment. He was always known by his nickname "Dutch." I don't know where that name came from but it really stuck. Around Garvin and Tracy he was always Dutch Olson. I am proud of all my brothers; I had it a lot easier than they did.

Those summers gave me more time to spend with my brothers and that was always fun. They taught me how to ride bike and they also let me drive their car around out in the fields so I could learn how to use a stick shift. I was always afraid of their dog Rover. There was no indoor plumbing so going to the outhouse was always tricky if the dog was around. Marvin would drive an old car in and out of the ditches. It had no body to it – just some flat boards to sit on and I would ride back there. I was a little scared sometimes, but it was fun. When Uncle and Auntie weren't around, we sometimes did a few things they probably wouldn't approve of. My brothers attended a country school, District 72, which was not too far from their home. Their teacher's name was Miss Herd, and I can remember visiting school with them.

One day while Marvin was working on the old Model T Truck they had (he always liked tinkering with cars,) the wheel was spinning and it threw a stone right into his leg. He sent one of his brothers into the house to get some towels to use to stop the bleeding, but Mrs. Hanson, frugal as she was, sent out an old black rag. I still remember sitting in Dr. Valentine's office once while Marvin was having his leg tended to and watched the doctor pull out several inches of gauze which had been packed into the wound thereby allowing it to heal from the inside out. Those were the days before antibiotics so all things considered it turned out very well. Marvin was in high school at the time and I believe he stayed down at Emil and Johnnie's house but ate meals at Olaf and Marie's. That was fun for me having a brother so close. Then he would catch the school bus out on the highway by our house. One of the boys who was a good friend of his (Marvin Rialson) carried his books up and down the stairs between classes for Marvin since he was hobbling around on crutches. Thankfully that all cleared up in good shape. It wasn't the only narrow scrape Marvin was in either.

My Mother's Postcards

When my last brother Orlando died and we were going through all the things that were at the home we found a treasure: My mother had received many very beautiful postcards from an admirer, a fellow named Oscar. There were so many and she kept them all. Whenever he went anywhere he sent a postcard to her and for every possible holiday there was a card. Jonathan has scanned them all onto my computer now as a screen saver, and I can print off any that I want to and occasionally use them to send to family members for Valentine's Day, Easter, birthdays, etc. I commented to my nephew Eugene (we call him Buzzy) one day that my Dad didn't send her any and he said, "*He probably didn't need to.*" ☺ I am sure that was true.

The years at the home of Uncle Olaf and Auntie Marie on the small acreage near Garvin.
I always called them Uncle and Auntie. I am sure I had it a lot better than my brothers. When you think of Leonard being only 8 years old and the others not being much older, it must have been hard to be living with just a hired girl and a hired man who helped out part time. I only know the name of one hired man and that was Clarence Hanson (he later became a pastor in our synod) and his mother was the cook for a time. She was very set in her ways and very frugal – watching every spoonful of sugar the boys put on their cereal and I heard stories about this. She always carried her purse with her wherever she went, probably think-

ing those four boys were going to rob her or something. I am sure there wasn't much money in it since the wages for a hired girl (lady) were pretty meager in those days. I found one of Uncle's old account ledgers where it said the hired girl got $15 a month.

I had a good home there with Uncle and Auntie. They took good care of me. Here are some things I remember about those earlier days:

Uncle's farm was small – only 20 acres if I remember correctly. It was right on the edge of Garvin, Minnesota. He originally was farming a 160 acre farm but because of some stomach trouble (ulcers probably) he needed to rent out his big farm in order to reduce his workload or level of stress you would probably call it today. His renter's name was Arthur Holm. He was married and had a family and was an excellent renter. He made money for Uncle on that farm as well as for himself since some years later he was able to go out and buy his own place. I can remember him coming up to Uncle's with a lumber wagon full of corn in the evening after he had gotten done picking corn. He needed a little corn for feed for the animals. We had a corncrib and there was a corn grinder which I would sometimes use to grind corn for feed. It was sort of a fun job – just had to be careful not to stick you hands down in there when the crank was turning. I was reminded of that quite often.

I spent most of my years from the age of about 4 until I went to Bethany for college in 1944 with Olaf and Marie on this small acreage. You oldest children would remember it but not Joel. I hope Jonathan remembers it a little.

On this farm he had a small red barn where he milked two cows; adjoining the barn was a chicken coop. Next to the barn was a very tall windmill which pumped cold water into a tank for the cows. There was also a water cooler out there where the cream can could be immersed in the cold water thereby keeping the cream sweet for a few days before taking it to the creamery. There was also a small red pig house, a red corncrib and a small red garage which was adjoined to Uncle's shop. As a child I spent quite a bit of time in the shop. I loved to use Uncle's tools and try to build things. I really liked to make wood curls with the plane. He also had a nice big drill which was mounted on the workbench so I drilled all kinds of holes in things.

Then, of course, there was the house which had two bedrooms, a bathroom, living room, dining room, kitchen, vestibule (is that a Norwegian word?), and a sun porch in front where I often sat on the steps and looked out at the cars driving by on Highway 59. I knew they had free shows up in Garvin and I always wished I could go; sometimes I would get to go with John and Elma and their kids. It was lots of fun. Later on when I could drive I was allowed to drive downtown to Garvin by myself. I liked going to Morgan's Café and ordering a Pepsi since those bottles were twice as big as the Coke bottles. What a treat!

There was also a full basement where we stored apples, potatoes and carrots which we raised on the farm. We picked the apples and wrapped each one in a sheet of paper from the Montgomery Ward Catalog to preserve them. The carrots were packed in a large crock full of sand and the potatoes were placed in a big pile. There was a special vegetable cellar for these products which had a dirt floor and was dark.

There was one part of the house that had many treasures and that was the attic. I spent lots of time up there. There was a stairway from my bedroom closet that went right up there. I remember one time I lost my glasses and later found them on the attic steps. There was also a trap door going up into the attic from the kitchen. It made it much easier to move some of the larger items up there. One treasure I had in the attic was a replica of the Lindbergh home which my Uncle Elmer built for me. It was complete with a yard and little trees and the window from which the Lindbergh baby had been kidnapped was pointed out to me. That was, of course, big news way back then. Unfortunately in later years when Iona[4] took over that home (Uncle Olaf's) I did not get to see it anymore. I don't know what happened to it.

I was talking with Eldora a couple of weeks ago and she mentioned how much fun we had playing in the attic up at Auntie and Uncle's. I had forgotten about that. I believe when the grandparents on both sides of the family were all gone and their homes had to be cleared out for new tenants, Olaf and Marie stored those things that no one in the families wanted or had room for in their own homes. That's what made the attic such a "treasure house." There were beautiful trunks from Norway filled with gorgeous dresses and hats, men's black derby hats, and some

---

4   Iona was not mentioned earlier but I will refer to her briefly here. She was adopted by Olaf and Marie. There was some relationship to her in the family but whatever that was I am not sure. They took her in and I must say a lot of grief came with it.

shoes. As I have had opportunity to look at some of the old photos I could tell our parents, aunts, and uncles liked to dress up and have their pictures taken. There was one trunk which was quite large. It was painted with sort of dull blue paint and also had rosemaling on it. That trunk would be worth a fortune nowadays. It was sold along with other treasures from the attic when Iona had an auction and luckily a relative of ours, Lennor Bakken from Walnut Grove, purchased it for I believe $35. What a deal! I was so happy it stayed in the family. My grandmother on my mother's side was a Bakken so I am sure it came over with her when she came with her father (Johannes), sister (Annie Bakken Rudd), and brothers (Albert and Ole). The trunk has the name Bakken inscribed on it. The Bakkens came from a farm in the Gudbransdal Valley near the city of Kvam. When Marie and I were in Norway in 1997 we visited this farm.[5]

Also up in the attic was another trunk from the Olson side of the family. This trunk we have in our family room downstairs and we all regard it as a treasured keepsake from the past. The inscription on it says "Ole Gulliksen Büer" Til Tracÿ Minnesota, Lÿond County, Nort Amirikka. I have some chairs I am using around my kitchen table that came from that attic.

I had lots of fun with my cousins when we would get together. Eldora and I are so close in age – we were like sisters. I really loved it when I got to go down to John's (my mother's brother) and Elma's (my dad's sister) since they had so many children (Kenneth, Myrtle, Vivian, Ruth, Orvin, Eldora, Maurice, and Viola) and we had a great time

5   Check my 1997 Christmas letter for more details.

playing there. We loved playing house out in the wooded area behind their house. We made a lot of mud pies. Our house in the woods meant a lot to us and we really worked at keeping it nice.

Occasionally some of my cousins would come up to Olaf's and we would have a tenting party. Uncle had a tent which we pitched right outside his bedroom window. I guess we weren't too brave were we? It was a lot of fun. I also had a girl friend from school who was about a year younger than I was. I would stay overnight at her house and she at mine. Her name was Betty Nelson. They had a lake called Long Lake on their farm where we would go fishing quite a bit. We would stay down there all day and bring all kinds of food to eat. We would catch bullheads. Her older sister Delpha would sometimes come down with us and I remember she would cut up frogs to use for bait. I could never do that but then she became a nurse so I guess it didn't bother her. I was able to thread on angle worms though - something I don't think I would like to do today. I had a lot of fun at the Nelson's and stayed overnight there every once in awhile. They lived about a mile and a half from Garvin so if I went home from school with Betty it was quite a walk. The Nelsons were also distant relatives of ours, second cousins or something like that. They had a beautiful home and lots of apple trees. I was treated royally the times I spent there.

I also liked to play with my dolls in the house. I had a corner in the living room underneath the library table which I used for my dollhouse and I spent a lot of time doing that. My Mother had my Aunt and Uncle buy a doll and buggy for me before she died. I don't know if I got it before she died or shortly after. I had other dolls also though - one was a Betsy-Wetsy doll. You fed her water with a little bottle and she wet her diaper.

Emil and Johnnie

Perhaps this would be a good place to reminisce a little about Emil and Johnnie. Emil was my father's half-brother and Johnnie was his full brother and also a brother of Olaf and Elma, of course. Johnnie was a very fastidious housekeeper. There wasn't much furniture in that house but one thing Johnnie possessed was an Edison phonograph player with a full set of records. They had one of those old couches which had the headrest built right into the makeup of the couch. I would lie on that and ask Johnnie to play records for me which he gladly did. I remember so well listening to "It's Three O'clock in the Morning " and also a whole lot of hymns. Another piece of furniture which they had was a large Philco radio. They went all out for a large radio like people do today with a television set. If the radio wasn't working Olaf would have to try and get it fixed or if all else failed get them a new one. Emil was a worrier and perhaps Johnnie, too. Emil was very good to me and gave me a quarter or some piece of change every time I walked by the house. He kept a lookout for me and came and visited with me a little bit on my way home from school and always with a little money in his hand. When he would run out of change my Uncle Olaf would have to bring him a new supply. Olaf had charge of his money since Emil was not able to take care of his finances. The "Crash" that happened during the Depression was very hard on both of those fellows as it was on an awful lot of people.

I had the job of walking down to Garvin and buying groceries for Emil and Johnnie once a week without fail. They had a little basket which I carried and sometimes it got a little heavy. But Johnnie always said, "*There's not so much heft to it.*" He was as fussy about writing out his list as he was about housekeeping. He would write it over and over if he didn't feel it was neat enough. I went down to Holden's Grocery where the owners owed Emil money. No money would change hands - they would just deduct the price of the groceries from what they owed Emil. I don't know if their debt ever got fully paid or not. Oh yes, they always told me that I should have a nickel's worth of candy for doing this little chore and that amount too was deducted from the store owner's debt. So I came out just fine.

October 22, 2004
Here it is October of 2004 and I am just getting back to my journal. I just retired at the end of August from 28 years of working at the seminary and synod offices. Who would have believed that I would be working that many years? I loved my work though and am glad that I was able to work that long. From there I moved over to the Ottesen Museum where I worked a lighter schedule.

Chores on the Farm
Every morning when Uncle was done milking he brought the pails of milk into the basement through the outside basement entrance. He had fixed up kind of a unique door opener for that which I saw this summer is still being used today. It was a pulley on a rope which made the door much lighter to open. My bedroom was directly above the base-

ment where the cream separator was. Whenever I heard the crank start to turn I had to jump out of bed and go down and help with the separating. The crank turned rather hard at first and then it got easier. When you got it up to a certain speed a little bell would ring and that was a sign that you could turn on the spigot so the milk and cream would start to come out. There was not as much cream as milk, of course, so we did not need a very large jar to catch it. There would be quite a bit of milk, however. We would first take some off to use in the house and I believe the rest went out to feed the pigs. The cats in the barn had already had their portion since Uncle saw to that early on. Sometimes he would squirt it directly into their mouths. Sometimes there would be little calves in the barn and we had to teach them how to drink milk after they were weaned from their mother. This we did by holding our fingers in their mouths and their heads down in the milk pail. This was kind of fun since it always tickled my fingers. The cream that we didn't use was taken to the creamery in Garvin where you got paid a certain price depending on how much butterfat was in it. The more butterfat the bigger the paycheck. Uncle was highly respected in the community and in the little village of Garvin. He served on both the Creamery Board of Directors and the Elevator Board of Directors.

Washing the separator was quite a job since there was a whole row of metal disks which had to be washed along with all the other parts of the separator. My Aunt Marie always did this and in the summer she had a bench out back of the house where she did the washing and let it air dry out there. I was glad I never had to wash the separator. One Sunday afternoon when our minister and family from Tracy Church were invited out to dinner, his two little boys who were quite the rascals poured sand into the separator. One turned the crank while the other poured in the sand. That same day they let the pigs out of the yard so they went out on the highway. They also threw the cats into the water tank and drowned them. What a day that turned out to be!

Sometimes I would mow the lawn with a push mower. The lawn was not terribly big but it was quite a job especially on hot days. I would also help in the garden which was a ways down behind the barn in the corner of the field. I guess it was good ground for a garden. We had several apple trees and a whole lot of rhubarb plants - too many. Sometimes people would drive by and come in and see if they could have some. We were happy to give it away.

Of course I helped with the dishes and cleaning of the house. I did the dusting and straightening up. I never liked things getting cluttered and I still don't like that although it has a way of happening quite often. I don't remember helping much with the cooking. About the only cookies we made were sour cream sugar cookies and they were good. Auntie was a pro at making those. They were kept in large jars in the basement where they stayed pretty fresh. She also was very good at making angel food cakes – all by beating and beating the egg whites with a hand beater. I believe we also had ginger snap cookies but Elma was the pro at making those. She was a terrific cook and baker too, as well as my Aunt Marie. Aunt Elma worked very hard raising such a large family without the conveniences that we have today.

Most certainly she was one of my favorite aunts and highly respected by everyone.

Another job that I had was on wash day. We had a Maytag washer down in the basement but had to heat the water on the cook stove upstairs. The fire really had to get going before putting the wash boiler on. The boiler was copper - now they are a collector's item. (In fact they use one at our Timber Lodge Restaurant here in Mankato which they keep filled with beautiful red delicious apples as a parting treat for their customers.)[6] We took the top burners off the stove so the fire would come directly under the boiler. I had to pump water to fill pails from the pump out in the vestibule (the entry) and pour them into the boiler until it was filled. I don't remember if they let me carry the hot water downstairs or not. I am sure I didn't when I was little but maybe later on I did. My aunt would wash clothes and run them through the ringer into the first tub of cold water where I had to stomp them up and down with a stomper. Then there was one more rinse tub of water which contained a little Mrs. Steward's Bluing. Supposedly this made the clothes a little whiter. I would also stomp them in this tub and when that was finished they were finally rung out in a basket and hung out on the clothesline especially in decent weather. Otherwise they were hung on a wooden rack which we would set over the floor furnace. Out on the front porch we had lines where we hung some as well, and they usually froze out there in winter so we would bring them in when the others on the rack were dry and then dry these. We just had to keep on until we got it all done. Sometimes it took days. I didn't like doing that

6   Unfortunately that restaurant also closed in 2009 or '10 due to the economic crunch.

job. Ironing was a big job since we had those flat irons that we heated on the stove and picked them up with a handle that attached to them. We could iron and iron until the iron lost too much heat and then exchange for another flat iron from the stove. We also used these flat irons to wrap in newspaper and put in our beds during the wintertime to keep our feet warm.

Wintertime brings to mind the unpleasantness of jumping out of bed in the cold. Hopefully Uncle would have the furnace going and I would run into the dining room where there was a floor furnace and stand over that to get dressed. In those days we had ridiculous garter belts which were like harnesses to put on and they had a tendency to get all tangled up. These were attached to our cotton stockings which we pulled up over our long underwear. Of course, there was no such thing as slacks – we wore dresses.

Uncle was such an ingenious person, though, that we actually had quite a modern house back in the early 30s. That floor furnace was really something in those days, and not only that, we had a bathroom. I think at first the toilet was one of those chemical jobs but later we got the works – a stool that flushed and a bathtub and sink. No hot water in there yet but that came later. We had running water in the kitchen. Uncle could figure out most anything. The vestibule[7] which was the first room you entered from the back door had a pump in it. There was a cistern outside the door which was the gathering place for rainwater and that's where we got our soft water for washing clothes. The

7   In the dictionary it says that a vestibule is a passage between the outer door and the interior of the building. That's exactly what it was. So I guess it's not a Norwegian word.

pump usually needed to be primed. In later years we also got a refrigerator which was in the vestibule and also a gas stove. In the kitchen was a Copper Clad range that was a beautiful peach-colored stove. It had everything – two warming ovens over the stove itself, a large oven for baking, and a reservoir. The reservoir kept water warm which we could use for washing dishes. I used to sit on a little stool beside the reservoir and wipe dishes while Auntie washed. It was kind of a cozy little nook.

Sundays.
We didn't get a Sunday paper but Johnnie did and since he didn't read the funnies I was allowed to go down every Sunday and get the funnies to bring home. I looked forward to that. I believe we got a daily paper, however. Uncle always wanted to keep up on the news. I remember him listening to the news on the radio regularly, and at 10 o'clock p.m. they always went to sleep listening to Cedric Adams. He was a real radio figure in those days. I can still remember his voice. People would say you could see the lights go out all over Minnesota at 10:15 every evening after Cedric Adams was over.

On Sundays we always went to church - first either to the chapel in Garvin or to Höland Lutheran Church. Then in about the later 1930s came a split in the congregation. The people who followed the old truths formed a new church, Zion Lutheran, in Tracy. That is where I was confirmed on June 28, 1942, by the Rev. Milton Otto. Rev. U. L. Larson had left a couple of years before.

Piano Lessons

I began taking piano lessons when I was about halfway through grade school. My teacher's name was Miss Freeman. One day she brought a picture of her class when she graduated from school and wanted me to pick out the one I thought was her. The one I picked out wasn't her and she was kind of hurt because she said that was a girl nobody in the class liked too much. Too bad, she shouldn't have asked me to pick. I liked her for a teacher though. I had really taught myself to play before I took lessons. I had a book with one of those sheets with the staff and all the notes on it. If you lined it up just right with middle C you could learn how to play that way. I know I went all through that first book by myself. We had a recital every year up in the big town of Marshall in the basement of the Methodist Church there. I always got a little nervous getting up on the stage to play but as far as I can remember I don't think I goofed up too much. The other day, while doing spring-cleaning, I came across a copy of one of the recital programs. I remember I always got to go to the dime store in Marshall and buy a new ring for the occasion. Lots of evenings I am sure Olaf and Marie fell asleep listening to my piano playing.

As my piano playing progressed I was asked to perform at all kinds of social functions in Garvin. A lot of times I was called upon to play for showers in the Congregational Church. I played for our neighbor's daughter's wedding in that church. I also played in the chapel in Garvin which was affiliated with the Höland Church, a convenient place of worship for those living in the Garvin area. When there were bridal showers or Young People's Societies and they were hard up for entertainment they called on me. I hopped on the bench and played songs like "Home Sweet Home" and the "Sweet By and By." These were a big hit with the Congregationalists. I had a variation of "Abide With Me" which belonged to my mother and was quite a favorite. The first wedding I played for was when my brother Gerhard and Bernetta got married. This wedding took place in the parlor of the home where I was born.

Elementary School Days at Garvin Public School.

I went to the Garvin Public School which was directly across the pasture from Olaf's. He built a wooden stepladder so I could cross the fence without tearing my skin or my clothes. It also saved me quite a bit of time.

Melvina, 1937
11 years old

Before I go any further I must tell you what I did each day before I left the house. I can still see Auntie standing on the step and I said this little prayer, *"Dear Lord, please help me to be a good little girl for Jesus' sake, Amen."* I also had a spoon of Cod Liver Oil every day which probably did a lot to keep me in good health. I have a lot of perfect attendance certificates – I found seven in a box of mementos while I was spring-cleaning this year. Once in awhile I could follow the Cod Liver Oil dose with a white peppermint candy which Olaf had on hand.

My first and second grade teacher was a cousin of mine, Mabel Dalthorp. That was on my father's side. Her mother was probably his half sister. I went through all eight grades at Garvin Public School. It was a nice big brick building that had four classrooms and a basement with restrooms and lunchrooms. The janitor there was very good to us. His name was Christ Nelson. He built a balancing beam for us to walk on and also had chinning bars which we could raise and lower to suit our height. In the spring he had a big box kite which he took out and flew on the playground. We were always excited about that. In the winter he flooded over a skating pond for us. We had those old clamp on skates and skated during the recesses. We also had a teeter- totter, slide, and giant strides to ride on. We played a lot of softball, Prisoner's Base and Pump Pump Pullaway.

One trick we played on our teachers almost every year, and especially if we had a new teacher, was called "Peanut Shower." We would have it all arranged ahead of time so we brought money to go downtown and buy peanuts in the shell during our lunch hour. The janitor always diverted the teacher's attention so we could smuggle in our little bag of peanuts. Then at a previously designated signal we all took out our bag of peanuts and started throwing them at the teacher. This was quite shocking especially to new teachers, but they seemed to take it in stride. After it was over we all went to pick up the peanuts and put a lot on the teacher's desk and we each had plenty for ourselves which we enjoyed eating. I have never heard of any other school doing this. I don't know how it got started in Garvin, but it was fun.

Every Christmas we put on an operetta. I remember one of the classrooms was all set up with a stage and the necessary properties. When we had practices those of us who were not on stage sat in one of the other classrooms waiting our turn to perform. I don't remember much about the performances except that I think there was a lot of singing and, of course, all the parents came and enjoyed it very much - we thought anyway. We loved getting out of all the schoolwork to prepare for this annual festivity.

There was a County Superintendent of Schools named Jennie Frost. She would visit our school quite regularly and I remember how nervous the teachers seemed to get when she came around. I really think we had a pretty good school. We had to learn a lot of grammar - all the different forms of verbs, memorized all the county officials like the county treasurer, county assessor, etc. Of course we had history, geography, arithmetic, spelling, handwriting, and art. I never did very well at handwriting or art. We had to use those scratchy pens. We had a wooden pen holder and then bought the pen points which fit into them. So we didn't need to buy a whole new pen set - just the pen point which we dipped into the inkwell on our desk. If we jiggled our desk too much sometimes ink spilled over onto our books. I know if we were lucky enough to get to be chosen to fill the inkwells that was considered quite an honor. There was a big ink bottle with a long sort of hose coming out of it which was used for filling. Another thing that got passed around was the paste. We each had a little container where we kept the paste and there was a huge jar of paste in the closet from which we could replenish our supply when needed. Some kids loved the paste so much they ate it. Not me. There was absolutely no gum chewing in school.

I liked most of my teachers. There was one in the 5th and 6th grade that I didn't really like and I don't think I did my best in those grades. In the 7th and 8th grades I had my first man teacher, Mr. Butler. I really liked him and that's when I started taking an interest in arithmetic.

May Basket Day was fun. We each made May Baskets for all the others in our class and set them on their desks. The teacher usually got an extra specially made one. I know one of my classmates had a sister who was especially talented in crafts and she made some beautiful ones. Nowadays May Basket Day is almost a thing of the past. The story went that if you left a May Basket on someone's doorstep that person was supposed to run after you, try to catch you and kiss you.

Melvina
Confirmation Day

Graduation from grade school was a big event in Garvin. It was held on the stage of the Congregational Church in Garvin. We had very nice graduation invitations complete with name cards. I still have mine. Today very little is made of graduating from eighth grade.

High School Days at Tracy High School
I was pretty busy in the mornings making my own break-

fast of milk toast and cocoa which I had every day. Olaf got the fire in the stove going so I could make toast in the oven and heat up the milk on top of the stove. I still like milk toast to this day but don't have it much. After breakfast I would sit in front of the dining room window by Uncle's desk and look down the road for the big orange bus to come. My school bus was as big as the greyhound busses are today or nearly so. The Garvin bus was the biggest bus picking up students for Tracy High School. Our driver was Blackie Crause and he didn't stand for any shenanigans on his bus. There wasn't trouble like there is today on school busses. If anybody was fooling around he stopped the bus and the offender got a good talking to. I used to get off downtown in Garvin on the way home to save me from riding all the way around the route. I got home much sooner this way. Our bus stopped between the two grocery stores in Garvin and sometimes I would go in and buy a Mr. Goodbar for 5 cents to eat on the way home.

I loved algebra when I got to high school. I took that my freshman year and the next year I took geometry which I loved just as much if not more. I never seemed to care much for history or geography, but today I don't think I would mind studying those either. Other classes I really loved were typing, shorthand, and accounting. That's probably why I like being a secretary so much. It was considerably easier than teaching school. I have some good memories from my school teaching days and that's how I met Dad, so those days were meant to be as my life was heading in a new and wonderful direction. When I think back I know that God was in charge.

The Years at Bethany Lutheran College in Mankato

What comes naturally after high school is college and in the fall of 1944 I was off to Bethany. This was quite an experience for me. I remember Auntie Marie made a patchwork quilt for me to take along which I still have. I made a vanity out of two orange crates. They were double crates made of wood and when you placed a board over the top (leaving an opening between the two crates) and gathered a curtain around the whole thing it made a fairly decent little piece of furniture. It wasn't like it is nowadays when students come with all kinds of furniture, TVs, stereos, etc. There was only one phone in the dorm and we didn't have access to it. I can't remember ever calling home. Everything was done by letter writing. I discovered the other day that I have quite a stack of letters which my Aunt and Uncle wrote me and I am sure I wrote back. I took the "400" train home for the holidays or the few weekends that I was able to go home. I believe the "400" went from Chicago to Pierre, South Dakota. I must have taken a cab from Bethany down to the depot in Mankato. I can remember one time when I came into Garvin on the train; it was dark and very early in the morning. I had to walk home and I was scared to death. I was frightened because there was a man walking along the street and in those days I was deathly afraid of dogs, too, but I made it OK.

Since I was so interested in being a secretary I took accounting and typing along with the other courses I needed like religion, English writing and literature –we studied Shakespeare. I even took Latin which I liked a lot and got an A in it. Oh yes, I took piano lessons, of course. There was a lot of musical talent there and I got to hear a lot of good music and had some good friends who were wonderful musicians. My roommates were my cousins, Eldora and Mildred. We got along just fine. But it seemed I got a little homesick and at the end of the first year decided not to return to Bethany. My Uncle Olaf who was both on the Elevator and Creamery Boards in Garvin landed a job for me as bookkeeper at the Garvin Creamery. So after my first year of college I became a bookkeeper. I really liked that job and was pretty good at it, too. In fact, when the auditor came, I had found some errors the previous bookkeeper had made and he told my boss, "*She's a darn good bookkeeper.*" I also found a $60 mistake the lady at the bank had made when I made a deposit for the creamery one time and the people at the bank were so happy about it. It was in their favor.

Once in a while when people came in with their cream cans I had to weigh them up if no one else was around and take a sample of the cream, taste it, and dump it into the vat. From there it went into a big churn to be made into butter. One of the worst things that could happen was when a mouse had drowned in the can of cream which you just tasted. That happened to me one time.

As you can well imagine there was not much going on in Garvin except for the free outdoor movies that came in the summertime. The social life revolved around the church. We lived 10 miles from Zion Lutheran Church in Tracy and I loved it when I could go to the Young People's Societies, and also to choir practice. Sometimes I would drive the car and Aunt Marie would ride along and wait in the car until I was ready to go home. In those days we were pretty careful about not doing too much extra driving – especially during the war years when we had a "B" gas card which allowed us only so much gas a month. If you had a "C" card you could get a lot more gas but we didn't qualify for that.

Back to Bethany College

At the end of that year as a bookkeeper I decided that life in Garvin was kind of a dead end street for me. I had made a trip or two back to Bethany for certain occasions and our pastor encouraged me to go back to college. By the fall of 1946 I was back at Bethany – this time deciding to take teacher-training courses. I shared a large room with three other girls whom I never knew before – their names were Zona Meyer, Vicki Wohlfiel, and Vivian Cox. We got along well and one thing I can remember is that on St. Patrick's Day we all wore green dresses that we had made. We went out and bought some green material that came in a tube so all we had to do was hem it up, make openings for the armholes and have an opening for the neckline. We must have put a belt with it. I guess we drew attention to ourselves. That year I got into the Bethany Choir when Alfred Fremder was the director. It was wonderful to be in the choir under his direction. The choir tour that year brought us to Chicago. Some other girls and I got on the train and saw a little of the city. Another big thing for me that year was taking organ lessons. I loved it so much and practiced and practiced even taking the hour of the girl who came after me when she never showed up for her turn at the organ. This happened quite often. For the spring recital I breezed right through *Bach's Prelude in C Major*, all from memory. My teacher was happy and I was happy, too. That spring, 1947, I graduated from Bethany College and was on the honor roll. Of course all of us who were preparing to be teachers were excited to find out where we would go. As it turned out I was called to Norseland Christian Day School. That was pretty exciting and not too far away. I probably wouldn't have worked out in a German church in Wisconsin since I was a full-blooded Norwegian – born and raised in the Norwegian Lutheran Synod. And besides I didn't want to be tied down to be an organist every Sunday.

Teaching at Norseland Christian Day School

When I graduated from Bethany College (2 yrs.) in 1947, I received a call to teach at Norseland Christian Day School as was previously mentioned. I was very happy to receive this call. I knew quite a few people already from Norseland since they had also attended Bethany. The first year that I taught, the school was located about a mile from the parsonage. I stayed at the parsonage where Rev. Tweit lived with his family. His wife Delphine was an excellent cook, and I always enjoyed good meals with the family. They had six children, three of whom I had as pupils that first year. I usually walked the mile distance to and from the school. There was no indoor plumbing and the building was heated by a large stove with a big black jacket around it. Coal and wood was provided by the parents of the pupils and it was my job to start the fire every morning and get it warmed up before the children arrived. Upon seeing the stove I told Rev. Tweit I didn't know how to start a fire in that kind of stove and he said, *"You know how to light a match don't you?"* I learned how to get that stove going.

When the classroom was quiet in the early morning and after the pupils had left in the afternoon the mice would come out. Trying to keep that under control in such an old building was impossible – you just had to let them have their space. They would crawl up and down the cloth curtains that covered the bookshelves. When school was out I would throw scissors at them and they would just retreat a little ways and come right back. One morning there was a weasel in the first entry of the old school building. When the pupils arrived they thought it was great and one of them got after it with a bat. For drinking water two of the students would get to go to a nearby farm and carry a pail full of water to place in our water cooler that had a little spigot on it. I don't know if I drank much water those days. The mothers of the pupils took turns preparing the teacher's lunch bucket. I had pretty good lunches. I remember one dear lady so much, Cora Rodning, who made the most delicious peanut cake. I will always remember her not just for that but she was such a fine, loving Christian woman. Teaching all grades was a challenge and I worked hard at it. We didn't have any of the fancy equipment that is common nowadays but the pupils got a well-rounded education in a Christian school. It was kind of hard being stuck in the country without a car and having to ask for rides to places I needed or wanted to go. I want to mention that Mrs. Tweit, Delphine, was an excellent homemaker so I was well taken care of. It couldn't have been easy for a family with six children to also board the schoolteacher.

At the close of my first year of teaching I took my first trip to California. Clara Annexstad and I boarded the *California Zephyr* at Worthington, Minnesota, and we were on our way. I believe it took us about two or three days before we got to Oakland, California. I don't remember if there were any stops between MN and CA. One thing neat about the Zephyr was the vista dome car up above where you could go up and have a whole seat to yourself. We packed some food to take along but also ate in the diner a few times. Terry met me at Oakland which was north of San Jose by several miles. Clara got a job in an onion warehouse as a secretary. Those Italians working there got such a kick out of her strong Norwegian accent. I didn't get a job out there – I didn't try. I just stayed with Marvin and Terry and also spent some time with my Aunt Emma. It was a wonderful summer, but I needed to get back to my job as teacher at Norseland Christian Day School where I taught for two more years before being called to Mt. Olive Lutheran School in Mankato.

I was happy to move to Mankato where I could be in a city and have access to some places I needed and wanted to go. It was also easier to get home weekends since I didn't have to ask someone to bring me to St. Peter to catch the bus and then to pick me up again on Sunday evenings when I returned. I always shied away from asking favors of people. I still do.

The Courtship of Melvina L Olson and Theodore A. Aaberg

This afternoon, July 27, 2005, I decided to write on this subject. I can remember it pretty well, one of the most thrilling and important times of my life. I need to back-track a little. In the fall of that year, 1947, my school was supposed to host the Christian Day School Conference which consisted of teachers and pastors in our district. I was busy getting my little country school all decorated up so as to make a good impression on the visiting teachers and pastors, many of whom I knew. Also the ladies in the congregation were preparing a noon meal of fried chicken and apple pie. It turned out that there was a terrible snowstorm and the conference was cancelled. I remember being asked by Ted Aaberg, who was teaching at Saude Lutheran School, to write up something for our Christian Day School Bulletin, he being the editor of that publication. I wrote it up and he printed it in the next CDS Bulletin titling it *Apple Pie and Fried Chicken*. Our conference, which had been canceled in the fall, met the next spring, 1948. Ted Aaberg was there for that but we did nothing more than visit a little bit. It was two years later when we actually started dating.

I decided to insert in this spot a copy of what Dad had written re: our courtship only a short time before he died. No one could say it better than he did. I quote:

> *This story is set down for our children, and hopefully, under God's blessing someday, wives and husbands and children's children, for the gift of a pious spouse is God's blessing.*
>
> *I remember the first time I saw Mamma.* (As his sickness progressed and he got really weak he resorted to using the word Mamma which is what he also called his own mother.) *It was when she got up to play the hymn at the ELS Christian Day School Teachers' Conference at Norseland, the spring of 1947, where she was teaching. The meet-*

ing usually held in the fall, had been snowed out.

I was struck immediately by an indefinable feeling and by her great beauty. I remember thinking of her and feeling good all the way back to Saude, where I was teaching under Pastor Milton Otto.

One might ask: "Well, why didn't you write her, court her and marry her. I did, but first I had other plans and work. The Saude School, privately run, had grown clannish, and a stern rebuke from me brought the result the congregation took over the school and for many years had 100% attendance and 20 students or more, bringing great blessing to the congregation. An infatuation with a girl resulted in my offering to teach the Jerico School, if they would start one. This they did, although it must be said the school has never taken deep root, and has had only 10-15 or so students per year.

It was too bad Dad waited so long to write this story; this was as far as he got.

☙

Chapter Two

~ Marriage & Family ~

❧

Valentine's Day 2006

Now you can see I have not been very diligent about writing in my journal. But it bothers my conscience a little bit that I have been negligent since I feel I owe it to you my dear children and grandchildren to be more aggressive. Today being Valentine's Day, and since I am approaching the age of 80 I had better get on with it. Although in no way do I feel like I think an 80 year old must feel. In fact, yesterday when I drove over to New Ulm to visit Shawna and Jennie since Shawna had been involved in a car accident the day before, I was taken back a little when a very nice girl offered to walk up to the 3rd floor and bring Shawna down rather than my walking up there. Then I realized it's my age she's thinking about. But I assured her I could easily make the stairs.

In the fall of 1950 I began teaching at Mt. Olive Lutheran School in Mankato, having received a Call to teach there near the end of my three years at Norseland. I enjoyed my years at Norseland but it was nice to get into a city so I could get around to places I needed or wanted to go without asking people to drive me since I had no car. Also it was nice to have the companionship of friends and acquaintances that I knew from my college days at Bethany. My cousin Mildred Johnson and I shared a large room with Grandma Galstad, Milly's grandmother, on the main floor of Bethany College. (Grandma Galstad worked in the Bethany kitchen.) The Bethany Alumni Association held its yearly meeting at Bethany that fall in October.

Now to the Courtship: A couple of weeks previous to that I had received a letter from Ted Aaberg asking me out to dinner that evening when he came up for the meeting. By that time he had been ordained and installed as pastor of the Scarville/Center parish. Of course I accepted his invitation and was very happy and excited about it. I can still remember walking out to the main lobby at Bethany around 5:30 or so and he was there waiting for me. As I remember there were others standing around, probably figuring they had gotten in on something special, and they had. Dad was a real gentleman. I remember thinking his car was really nice – it was a tan Chevrolet I believe. (At that time I thought Chevrolets were the best since that's what I grew up riding in with Uncle Olaf.) Dad opened the car door for me and did all those nice things a gentleman is supposed to do. We went to a restaurant in North Mankato someplace on Belgrade Avenue. I don't remember the name of it and I am sure it isn't there anymore. I

even remember the dress I wore. I believe it was a black
dress. (Was I trying to be sexy or what?) Sometimes I
think I should have worn something else but this was my
best dress at the time. We had a good time and at the close
of the evening he brought me up to the hall leading down
to where my room was. (By the way, that room is now the
office of the President of Bethany College.)

It wasn't long until I received another letter from him asking me out to dinner again. And again I happily accepted.
He took me to the Elk's Club which was a rather nice little
restaurant underneath some other building downtown – I
believe it was under the old Ben Pay Hotel. Anyway, we had

Melvina L. Olson & Theodore A. Aaberg
the pictures they exchanged during their courtship

many nice meals there. It was kind of a private place. I felt
completely at ease being with him. I remember one time
early on when we were riding in his Chevrolet, he looked at

me and said, "*You are so easy to be with.*" I thought, that's a nice thing to hear. I remember early on he asked me about my parentage and I told the sad story about my mother dying of breast cancer when I was only four and my father having died of a "ruptured stomach" – (as reported in the Tracy Headlight Herald) when I was only 16 months old. (I didn't very often tell people about my heritage – it was too sad.) This time I thought it was important and it didn't seem to scare him off. It seemed that about every couple of weeks or more he wrote me and I always accepted his invitations. Soon he got to taking me to the movies and I remember the first one very well: It was a little scary, something about mountain climbing – still a favorite type of movie to watch. Anyway, this time he reached over and held my hand. I think our future together was sealed right then. I must have gotten goose bumps. It turns out that Hugo Handberg and his wife Harriet were sitting right be-hind us that evening but we didn't know it until the movie was over. I still have all the letters I received from Dad and I am sure I answered every one. He could be a little bit shy about some things and being pastor in that little village of Scarville he didn't want the postmistress to have too much to gossip about so I began writing and mailing in more business type envelopes and typing in the address. I doubt that put anything over on Lucille, the postmistress, though. But Dad liked getting my letters and I certainly liked get-ting his. It made my school teaching days much happier. One time when he came up we went to a musical or some such thing which was held at the auditorium of a public school. That was one of the few places I can remember that we went to together in public. I guess most evenings he wanted me all to himself so we went out to dinner, to the movies and just driving around in his "Chevrolet."

When he came to Mankato – usually on Sunday evenings – he quite often stayed overnight at the home of Rev. and Mrs. Christian Anderson. They were an older retired couple, very nice I might add, who lived on Center Street. I remember on one occasion I happened to be out for the evening not knowing that Dad was coming up. When I got in I got the message that he had been to our room looking for me. I was, of course, disappointed that I had not been home but I am sure he was, too - probably wondering what I could be doing out on a Sunday evening. After all there were a lot of other eligible young seminary students around and at that time we were not yet engaged, but he needn't have worried. Anyway, I called down to the Anderson's fairly early the next morning and we undoubtedly went out that evening. So I guess he had a rather lonesome evening but then maybe not since the Anderson's were such special people. I might add they attended our wedding and also were our guests at Scarville on at least one occasion. Dad told me they thought I was awfully busy after having three children in three years and that probably he should see that I didn't get too tired out. Weren't they sweet?

By the end of November, Thanksgiving time, I was home for the holiday when I received a phone call from Dad. He wanted to come up to Garvin for the weekend, or part of it. At that time I hadn't even told Auntie and Uncle about my being courted by a preacher, the Rev. Theodore Aaberg, after all it had only been a month. So I was reluctant to have him come before I had a chance to tell them about him.

I discouraged him. Now I wish I hadn't done that but I guess I was just too timid. In those days things were different than they are nowadays. He took it in stride, however, and it wasn't long before I did have him up to my home in Garvin. In fact, they even cooked lutefisk for him so it must have been close to Christmas. (I wonder if I ate any of it.) I still remember when they were passing it around the table and it came to Olaf first and Dad said, "*You help yourself.*" Olaf said, "*We want you to be first.*" It's funny the things you remember. I also remember that same evening Iona made an appearance. She had evidently gotten wind of his coming. I was so embarrassed to see her. She was in her usual obnoxious form. I was glad to have that over with and Dad didn't dump me even after meeting her.

I need to interject this here that he sent me a box of *Whitman's Sampler Chocolates* – and had it mailed to my Garvin address. Perhaps it came during Christmas vacation. I remember this: My Aunt Marie said: "*It is not proper to accept a gift from a gentleman friend that you can't eat if you are not engaged to be married.*" She fully approved of him sending me candy. And I must add that I got many more Whitman's Chocolates throughout the years.

Needless to say we went out many evenings - every week or two as often as he could get away from his parish. Knowing the small salary he received I wonder how he was even able to take me out to dinner and movies so much. I wasn't making much money either, maybe $80 a month. I can't remember what it was. I should have offered to pay for some of that eating out. If I had an apartment I could have cooked some meals for him when he came. But I really liked going out to the Elk's Lodge where he always took me.

Right before Christmas that year his father, Theodore Aaberg, Sr., died suddenly of a heart attack. I remember that Joe was at Bethany at the time and Dad drove up from Scarville one evening after hearing the news and together he and Joe took a train, I believe, to Seattle or Tacoma for the funeral. That was a sad time for them. I always wished I had known his father. I am sure he was a wonderful man and easy to get along with. On Dad's return trip from the funeral he brought me a beautiful silver bracelet. His brother Herman had given him a certificate to spend at a nice department store in downtown Tacoma and he used it to buy this beautiful bracelet for me. I still have it, of course, but from wearing it almost constantly it eventually wore thin some of the connecting links so I am not able to wear it any longer. Later he also gave me a necklace and earrings to go with it. While he was in Washington I had my tonsils out at the old Immanuel Hospital downtown. It was a miserable experience since they didn't put me under and I could feel all that cutting. I was sitting in a chair like a dentist's chair when they performed the surgery. I was supposed to get out the same day but because of too much bleeding I had to stay there at least overnight. What a thing to do over vacation! I was fortunate that Aunt Mabel lived in Mankato at that time and she was my nursemaid. When Dad got back to Mankato after the funeral he stayed at Mabel's a night since I was recuperating there. I also got to go home to Garvin for part of the Christmas vacation via Mabel's transportation. Mabel's house was a good place to hang out sometimes.

A few weekends Dad must have gotten a substitute preacher because we spent some time up at Olaf and Marie's. It was on one of those trips back to Mankato on an early Monday morning Dad asked me to marry him. I can still remember where it was – it was while driving up the hill by the Glenwood Cemetery. I said, "*Yes*" and he said, "*Say it again,*" so I did and then he said, "*I have found myself a wife!*" It was a very happy day! Then I had to hurry off to Mt. Olive for school and he had to return to his parish work down at Scarville. I remember running over to Mabel's house on Belle Avenue at the time and telling her – I don't know if I had time before school or had to wait until after school. I wonder how I did teaching that day. It was quite a day – a wonderful day! I was fortunate to have Mabel so close. Occasionally we have talked about Mabel and her sometimes-irritable ways but all in all she was good to me. I wish I had done more for her.

Along came spring and our relationship continued to flourish if I may use that word. On one occasion I took a bus to Albert Lea where Dad picked me up and drove me down to Scarville – my first trip down there. He lived in the upper floor of the parsonage and rented out the bottom to the principal and his wife of the Scarville grade school. Of course it would not have been proper for me to stay there with Dad then. He probably wanted to take me down to Scarville and see how I liked it. I was quite impressed with the house. (Joel probably doesn't remember anything about our home there but the rest of you children know it well.) He made arrangements for me to stay overnight with Camilla and Nels Faugstad. That was a wonderful place to stay. For some reason the service that Sunday was held in the auditorium of the grade school. It must have been a special church service for the circuit or something. I don't even remember anyone I met down there except for Camilla and Nels Faugstad. But you can bet there were a lot of eyes on me. I was a little shy about it all and those people were probably a little curious, too. I am much more outgoing today than I was then or I probably would have gone around shaking hands with people and introducing myself.

I want to tell you more about the weekend up at Olaf and Marie's when Dad got up the courage to ask them for my hand in marriage. It probably was in April 1951. Uncle Olaf was milking cows out in the barn when Dad approached him asking for my hand in marriage. Dad told me that Uncle gave his blessing and said, *"She's a good girl, take good care of her."* I imagine Dad promised he would. Then he came back into the house and asked Aunt Marie the same question. She was busy preparing breakfast and I know she was nervous as was Dad, but she gave her permission as well. I don't think I was nervous – probably one time I wasn't nervous; I believe after that we drove to Tracy where I sat in the car outside the Berger Jewelry store while Dad went in to purchase a ring for me. Perhaps he had already been there and picked it out. He must have because he came out with it and it was my size and everything. That was a great day. After we got back to the farm there was company there. My Uncle Carl and Aunt Rena and family had come visiting. Mildred was there also and I had a chance to show her my ring. Dad probably had to leave about mid afternoon and drive back to Scarville. After all, he did have a parish to take care of.

Then, of course, we had a wedding to plan. We couldn't set any date yet because Aunt Marie had been sick for quite some time with complications due to her diabetes. She had that sickness for many years. She was in and out of the hospital many times. Sometimes she was in the Tyler Hospital located in a small town west of Garvin which had the reputation of being a good hospital with good doctors. I took a week off from teaching at Mt. Olive to stay home with her for one week. Then she was transferred to the Colonial Hospital (part of the Mayo Clinic complex). Finally she was transferred to the Tracy Hospital since that was the one closest to Garvin and that is where she died. I believe it was April 20, 1951. It was a sad time for us. Dad had made trips to all of those hospitals to visit her. Olaf was especially lonely after that and wrote a poem in remembrance of her which I will enclose with this writing. He was sad too since I would be moving so far away after the wedding. At least it seemed far away in those days. I remember he once said he wished it was only as far as Marshall or something like that. The funeral was held in Zion Lutheran Church in Tracy where we were members. Uncle Olaf asked Dad to speak a few words at the funeral and he did that. In those days the body was brought to the home before the church service for one last visit where a short pre-service was held. I remember looking for Dad before we were ready to leave for the service in Tracy and found him out behind the barn in the cow pasture practicing his speech. I can't remember anything about it but I am sure it was good.

"In Memory of My Wife"

Forty-two years of happy life
We have lived together as husband and wife.
Each one pleased and satisfied.

In twilight after the setting sun
When our daily tasks were done
We would sit and talk awhile.

When a Bible passage she had read
And our evening prayers were said,
Then in each other's arms we rested.

Next morning before the stars faded away
We were up together for another day.
What a happy life we lived.

When out on our little walk,
She liked so well to stop and talk.
You could hear her charming laughter.

She loved to be out with me when she was well,
Such company and such a pal –
What pleasant memories.

Together we worked and played and planned,
But now alone again I stand,
In sorrow and despair.

When the sunset of life is drawing near,
The voice I loved so well to hear,
Now by death is stilled.

When on this earth no more I trod,
Together again we'll rest beneath the sod.
Till we hear that final call to live with Christ in Glory!

Olaf C. Olson

Wedding Plans

A few weeks after the funeral we decided we could now make plans for our wedding, and came up with October 8, 1951, as an appropriate time.

We were married on a beautiful fall day at my home church, Zion Lutheran, in Tracy, Minnesota.
Uncle Olaf escorted me down the aisle and gave me away. My cousin Mildred Johnson was my maid of honor and Joe Aaberg was Dad's best man. We only had those two attendants. Eugene (Buzzy) Olson was the ring bearer and Elizabeth Tweit was the flower girl. The local pastor, Rev. Stuart Dorr, was the officiant. Margaret Annexstad, a good friend and very fine organist from Norseland, played the organ and the Rev. Milton Tweit sang, *"Now Thank We All Our God"* and *"The Lord's Prayer."* Since I taught at Norseland for three years it was only natural that we would like to have friends from there included in our "big day." My brothers Leonard and Orlando were the ushers. All my family was there — aunts, uncles, cousins and friends and also several pastors and their wives were in attendance.

The reception was in the church basement as they all pretty much were in those days. Going to a hall someplace and having a dance afterwards would have been a definite no, no. However, I have enjoyed going to lots of wedding receptions and dances since then. I always wished I had learned to dance so I could participate. My brother Marvin was a great dancer and I should have learned from him while we were growing up but that, too, was a no, no, for me to learn to dance in those days. We did have a lovely reception and I had a lot of help from my cousins and aunts, especially Aunt Mabel, who poured coffee and helped with decorations. There was a program at the reception at which a few people spoke. The one I remember was Rev. Justin Petersen; he said he had tried to find out what the name Melvina meant. He couldn't find a meaning for the name but said it had a musical sound to it. Also Ruth and Elizabeth, the two young Tweit girls, sang a song. They were good little singers.

They did it a little differently in those days when it came to opening the wedding gifts. They were opened by some whom I had designated for this job and put on display right there in the church basement. That practice had both its ups and downs. The upside of it was that the guests could see the gifts before they went home. The downside was that we didn't get to open them ourselves, but it didn't really make much difference. It's awfully nice for the guests to get to see the gifts.

After the crowd had gone home Dad and I drove over to John and Elma's house where I had changed into my wedding gown before the service and where I now was taking it off again and getting into my going away suit and hat. And yes, I did say *hat*. I guess that was proper attire in those days. And so we were off for our honeymoon. Driving south on Hwy. 59 past Garvin we saw Uncle Olaf with the milk pail in his hands going out to milk the cows. I felt a little sorry for him. This began a new chapter in our lives and his. Our honeymoon took us to the Ozark Mountains down in Missouri. It was beautiful down there. We visited Mark Twain's home, the seminary in St. Louis where Dad had gone for one year, and many other wonderful places.

Coming back up to Iowa we stopped at Saude where Dad had taught and stayed with the Otto's for one night. We also went to Calmar and stayed one night with Dad's Aunt Ida and Uncle Herman Preus. After the honeymoon we went back to Garvin for a day or two and packed up some things that we could get into the car and were then on our way to our home in Scarville, Iowa, where all you children were raised – some for more years than others.

Dad carried me across the threshold as we came into the kitchen, as was sort of an unwritten custom you were supposed to do with your new bride.

Early years in the Scarville Parsonage
It was a huge house and we didn't have much furniture so housekeeping wasn't such a big deal as far as dusting, etc. It was a beautiful home that at one time had been owned by the banker of Scarville. It had two stairways – one from the front hall and one up from the kitchen. It made it kind of handy – especially if you wanted to avoid someone coming up the opposite stairs. We had a new stove and refrigerator that Dad bought from Landy Hardware in Lake Mills, Iowa. I remember we ate on a card table for quite a while. He also purchased a washing machine before we were married. We had those practical things. We had a couch which I brought along from my teaching days at Mt. Olive. I used it to sleep on in the dorm room that my cousin Milly and I shared with Grandma Galstad. The couch pulled out into a bed (not very comfortable), but it was something to sit on and helped to fill up the living room. Dad, of course, had a desk in his study and there was one of those old iceboxes from years back for the mimeo-

graph to sit on. It probably came with the house when he moved in. I had my single bed from home and a dresser which had been my mother's. Dad had a three quarter-sized bed and the mattress on it came from an old fold-up couch, I believe. We soon bought a full-sized bed which is the one we have in the extra bedroom downstairs. Some years later we were able to buy the beautiful bedroom set at a furniture store in Forest City which I use to this day and will always use.

Also I had a little table that came from Grandpa Johnson's house and now Jonathan has it. I had a sewing machine which I purchased with what little money I earned from teaching. That was really handy. I have always been proud of the fact that I have my mother's piano which my brother Gerhard was so kind to bring down in his truck shortly after we moved. ("Gay" was always so good-hearted to do things for others.) What a blessing that was! All of you had lessons at one time or another and two of you got to be outstanding musicians and some not so much, but it is a gift that you all have to one degree or another, and it is something to be proud of. I am proud of all of your play-ing. Too bad my mother could not have lived to hear the beautiful music our family could make - starting out on her piano which my father bought her.

Dad used the money he got from renting out the lower level of the parsonage before we were married to buy bush-es for landscaping the parsonage. I know Dad got $70 a month from Scarville and $80 a month from Center when we were first married and for some years after that. But I must mention that we also got the three festival offerings each year (Christmas, Easter and Pentecost). At that time the parishioners marched around behind the altar where there was a dish on one side for the organist's salary and another on the other side for the pastor's salary). These offerings helped out, but things were pretty tight.

Shortly after we came to Scarville we proceeded to decorate the rooms downstairs. We went to Albert Lea and picked out some wallpaper. I had seen some I really liked in the Skinner Chamberlin Department store that I thought would be perfect for the living room. One of the walls was a solid green and the other walls were a coordinating paper in sort of a square design of the same color green and white. It was quite heavy paper and kind of difficult to put on. I wasn't much help to Dad putting that on. It was working with that paper I first learned that Dad could get a little impatient at times. I never saw that side of him while we were dating. In the dining room we picked out a yellow flowered wallpaper and in the downstairs bedroom which later became the family room we had a green ivy design. That was a poor choice now that I think of it because that was such a dark room. My favorite paper was always the living room, and which cost the most I am sure. We had white princess style curtains in that room which really set it off but they were a bear to iron because of all the ruffles. One thing that was strange in those old houses was the ceilings were also papered. What a job that was and I remember Harry Olson coming over to help with that. He was quite a wallpaperer.

The kitchen was also being remodeled by Iler Iverson. Little as I knew about cooking I had to prepare meals for him and his helper right after we were married. We got some nice cupboards put in as well as a nice red Formica countertop and maybe new linoleum — I don't remember. Little by little I learned to cook. Being a pastor's wife we often had to entertain guests – for meals as well as overnight. Usually they were pastors who were coming down for whatever reason. I do know it wasn't because we had a comfortable bed or that my cooking was so great. Certain people I remember coming whom I really enjoyed and they were Rev. and Mrs. Christian Anderson, good friends of Dad's as well as quite prominent people in the synod. In fact, Dad stayed at their home on Center Street in Mankato when he would come up to court me while I was teaching at Mt. Olive School (1950-51). Mrs. Anderson liked to braid rugs and she made us two beautiful braided woolen rugs from some woolen garments I gave her. We had them on our hardwood floor in the living room until the Center/Scarville Ladies Aids put in carpeting for us sometime later. They had beautiful oak floors in that house and I didn't appreciate them at the time since they took quite a bit of care when it came to cleaning and waxing them. Lots of elbow grease was used on that process. We were, of course, preparing for an open house at the parsonage. We felt we owed it to them since they had provided us with funds to do some redecorating.

I remember staying up until 4 o'clock in the morning the night before the open house which was on a Sunday. Some of the ladies offered to bring in cakes for coffee and that was a godsend. I don't know how I ever would have gotten that done. I have a guest book with the names of all who attended. Each congregation also had a reception for us shortly after we were married. **I need to add this for Joel's benefit:** After the Scarville reception a friend of Dad's and a member of the congregation, Ray Dale, approached him about the possibility of going out pheasant hunting. Dad took him up on it so I had to catch a ride home from the reception with Marybelle and Iver – pack up all the presents and everything, I should have teased him about that but I didn't.

For entertainment we usually went calling on certain members in the evening. I think especially of the Faugstads - Mr. and Mrs. Nels Faugstad and Arne. Dad always got to play whist with the men and I visited with Mrs. Faugstad who always made a delicious lunch of ice cream, homemade cookies and coffee, of course. In Scarville coffee was the common drink or Kool Aid for the children. During the holidays we usually got many invitations out for dinners. Homes that were on our regular list for a big dinner were Nels and Camilla Faugstad, Conrad and Esther Faugstad and Harry and Signe Olson. At Harry's we would get a small glass of red wine before our meal and that was really a celebration. Not like nowadays when wine has gotten to be a pretty common beverage. We didn't have much money to work with. If we hadn't gotten some meat from time to time and eggs I don't know how we could have made it. Dad made some visits to members in Bricelyn who would usually send home eggs in a big oatmeal box and there would be a $20 bill on top. That was really something. But I guess not many of the members were exactly rolling in the dough either.

I know I didn't buy many new clothes except when it came time to buy maternity clothes. For the first Christmas I purchased some flannel and made Dad a pair of pajamas for a Christmas gift. He gave me a couple of wooden salad bowls and a red shadow box which looked nice on our living room wall. We paid our own utilities except for the telephone which was a pretty small expense anyway. I think they figured since we had to call long distance across the state line to visit parishioners they should pay that expense. Dad and Harry Olson hauled coal from the railroad cars down by the tracks for our furnace. I remember Dad would throw open the doors and windows early in the morning to air out the house before turning the furnace up. We all stayed in bed until that was over.

We enjoyed the little town of Scarville and became good friends with our neighbors and others in that little community-- even though most of the town's people belonged to the (other) Lutheran church and we to the conservative Synod church as we were known. I know you children had some close relationships with other children there. Teddy with Daniel Sabo, Sarah with Linda and Diane Smith, Marie with Greg Wuerflien and Julie Brekken, and Jonathan with Randy Escherich and Larry Albertson. Joel was only three when we moved from there so he didn't have much of a chance to latch onto a playmate there. Harry and Signe with their children Lois and Steven lived across the tracks right outside of town so there was quite a bit of going back and forth to their house. I know the children organized a Club of some sort and met down by the creek. We made good friends with those people in Scarville. They were kind to us.

There were two grocery stores in town – Reiso's and Veryl Meyer's. We bought a lot of our groceries there but whenever Dad would go to a larger town like Lakes Mills, Forest City, or Albert Lea he would often come home with groceries from there. He was always good at picking out some things to add to our "pantry." I liked it when Dad did that. We got some things I probably didn't think we could afford.

The Beginning of our Family.
Although the parsonage was pretty empty for almost a year after we were married, on **September 16, 1952, Theodore Edward was born.** He came a month early. The ladies in the two congregations had planned a baby shower to take place at the parsonage. Well, here came Teddy and we had not had the shower yet. I remember one of the members at Center who was supposed to bring the baby basket hurried over with a nice bassinet. I think it was a daughter of Mr. And Mrs. Elmer Branstad. I must have had a few baby clothes on hand since we got through until the shower which was held shortly after we got home from the hospital. So now we had three instead of two living in that large house. What a joy that was! Of course, the whole town of Scarville was excited because by that time we had gotten pretty well acquainted with our neighbors. I think I was a pretty worried mother for a while – always afraid he would catch a cold or something. But it was lots of fun having a baby. We got a nice bathinette from Dad's sister Ida. I really loved having that. We got along fine and it was fun bundling him up and taking him to church, Ladies Aid, Dorcas Society, etc. The congregation was really good to us. I remember shortly after Teddy was born I got sick

with a breast infection and Dad was scheduled to go and preach somewhere down in Iowa so he made arrangements for me to stay out at Nels and Camilla Faugstad's. That was a great place to stay since she was a nurse and a very good one. Many times we had called on her about health questions we had. I remember one time I had a package of raw pork chops on the counter and Teddy sank his teeth into it. I was petrified knowing you shouldn't eat raw pork. I remember trying in vain to get him to throw up but to no avail. I don't think he had really eaten any of it and now he is 54 years old so it was OK. He used to pull all the kettles out of the part of the stove where they were kept and then tried to crawl in himself. Another trick he had that used to give John Larson, one of the neighbors, a chuckle was when he wanted to get in from the little fenced in play yard outside and was too short to reach the handle of the screen door, he got down on his knees and stuck his little finger in the bottom right hand corner where there was a small opening and got in that way. He did not like it when Dad was gone for a day or two. One time he got hold of Dad's pipe and hung on to that while he was sleeping – this was his makeshift security blanket I believe.

It wasn't too long before **Sarah came along. She was born on October 8, 1953,** which was on our 2nd wedding anniversary. Our family was growing. We thought it was wonderful to have both a son and a daughter. Now we had to get another crib. While I was in the hospital with Sarah, Teddy was taken care of by Signe and Harry Olson. He learned to walk while down there so I missed out on those first few steps. Sarah was a good baby who liked to suck her thumb, and in the morning when I woke up she would be wide-awake but very content as long as she had her thumb. Teddy would stand up in his crib on one side of the bedroom and look across to Sarah's crib and say, "*Saah*" as best he could. I think he liked having a sister. It was fun having a little girl to dress up and take to church and Ladies Aid. Those were the two places we mostly went in those days unless we made a trip to one of the Faugstad's for an evening visit where we always enjoyed a good lunch, and I think they enjoyed having us.

Then in another year, 1954, **Marie came along** to join the family. **She was born on November 23, 1954.** Now with three children we really felt like we had a family – three children – wow! I know we didn't buy a 3rd crib. I don't remember how we did it, but Teddy must have gone into a small bed. I remember one night while I was up with Marie sitting in a rocking chair in the living room in the wee hours of the morning, someone came thumping up on the front porch and rang the bell. It nearly scared me out of my wits. It turned out to be some fellow driving through Scarville who was looking for Rake, Iowa. We were the only house in town with a light on at that time of the early morning, of course. Dad must have come to the door and given him directions. Marie had her precious blanket which Emma and Lena Sande made for her. It was flannel, stuffed with some soft wool I believe, and tied with pink yarn. She had that with her everywhere she went. She carried it around town and it would get dirty so I had to wash it and little by little it practically disintegrated. I believe we still have a very small portion of it here someplace. It was her "security blanket." Being the third child she probably needed something like that.

Needless to say, I was pretty busy. Every Sunday I got them ready for church and took them to Ladies Aids and Dorcas Society regularly. I enjoyed the Ladies Aids and once I got there I had lots of help. I remember that Marie, when she got a little older, sat with Nora Stephens in church for quite awhile until she was just tired of doing that and insisted on coming back to sit with me. I remember Sarah sitting with Hilma Dale one time and she was crying and crying. I was up playing the organ. I didn't know what to do since Hilma wasn't taking her out. I think I had to finally leave the organ and take her out and put her in the car. Then I came back in and told someone to go out there and watch her since I needed to stay at my post on the organ. What a day! I also played the organ in Center for about four years. I don't know exactly which years those were but some people there had to take care of the children while I did that. That was the fate of many a pastor's wife especially if she was able to play the organ or piano – whatever they had.

Once in awhile we went to Albert Lea shopping and that was a big deal. Sometimes we would even go someplace for supper before we came home. Money was very tight, of course, as it usually was for pastors so we had to be wise spenders. With my upbringing during the Depression I was used to being thrifty. And, of course, so was Dad – even more so.

Trip to visit Grandma in Washington
When Marie was less than a year old we took a trip out to Parkland, Washington. What a trip that was! We have a cute picture of Teddy and Sarah with their little suitcases as we were ready to leave. I am wondering if we stopped

to visit my Uncle Melvin and Aunt Emily on the way who lived in Colorado Springs. Dad had a new Pontiac which was a deep rust color. As I remember we had no car trouble, but it was hard traveling with three small children when there was no such thing as disposable diapers. I remember Dad built a little potty chair which we kept in the back on the floor. Of course we had to have baby formula, too. Staying at Grandma's house was not without its problems. We all slept in one room upstairs and Marie slept on an old plastic davenport which was kind of rounded on top so it was not something easy for her to get used to. But it was the best that could be done under the circumstances. While we were there Marie came down with a fever and we had to take her to the doctor where she got a shot of penicillin. That took care of that. It was nice to spend some time with Dad's brothers Paul and Randolph, and also Ernie and Ingeborg Quick and their two children (Ted and Tom) who were about the ages of Teddy and Sarah. We enjoyed visiting the Quick family up in Morton for one night. It was a beautiful trip with a great view of Mt. Rainer along the way.

After staying with Grandma for a time we were off to California. First stop was Yuba City where Dad's sister Ida and her husband Bernie lived. I believe we stayed there one day and from there we took off for San Jose to spend time with my brother who was, of course, your uncle Marvin, and his lovely wife, Terry. Christine was about the same age as Teddy, but I am not sure how old Nancy was at that time. We did enjoy our time there a lot. We had more comfortable sleeping quarters there. In California we had our first look at a TV. I remember my cousin Alice volunteered to take care of Marie, she being only one year old, while the rest of us went on some kind of a tour. When we came back from our outing Marie was sitting in front of the television and I dare say hadn't missed us at all. What a great babysitter. It all started in California, and she still loves watching TV.

Grandma Aaberg came to visit occasionally. She and Dad did not see eye to eye on some theological issues; she loved to debate those issues and that sometimes was stressful. She did at times send some nice gifts in the mail to the children.

During this time Dad was busy with his two congregations, work on our synod publication, the Lutheran Sentinel, and on various boards of the Synod. His colleagues began to realize the special talent he had for writing as well as being a great preacher and so he got many extra jobs to do such as preaching for special occasions, preparing papers for synod meetings, circuit meetings, and committees to name a few. All of which he enjoyed I am sure. He was always very faithful about visiting the sick and shut-ins and doing whatever errands he could do for them like taking them to buy groceries or to the doctor or whatever.

Trip to Colorado
In 1959 we took another family vacation having just three children at that time. We went to Colorado Springs, Colorado, where I had family to visit, my Uncle Melvin and Aunt Emily. Melvin was a construction worker - one job he had that I know of was putting up mailboxes at the Air Force Academy there. We stayed in a motel since they had a small home and we didn't want to impose upon them

because of their age, but they treated us royally. Some places remembered from that trip are the Broadmore Skating Arena which you still hear about when it comes time for the Winter Olympics and other big skating events, also The Garden of the Gods and Pikes Peak. Marie remembers hearing the ice cream truck driving around playing music to attract little customers.

Scarville Christian Day School
I had left this blank for awhile and thought I would fill it in later. I want to say that Scarville Church had a Christian Day School years earlier but was closed due to the lack of pupils. This was during the time that Justin Petersen was pastor. He, too, was a strong promoter of Christian education. Now with our family ready for school Dad wanted a Christian school for our children as well as the children of the congregations. He was able to convince the Scarville Congregation that the school should be reopened. Just as our children were of school age the doors were opened. Teddy and Sarah were ready for school. There were several Faugstad children who were also of school age. Dad drove out to Center Congregation and picked up pupils at the homes of a couple of families there who attended as well. He really was happy to get the school going again after being closed for several years. When he came home that night after the meeting he called Rev. Norman Madson, Sr. to tell him the good news about the Scarville school opening. Rev. Madson had already gone to bed but he said he didn't mind being awakened to hear such good news.

On March 7, 1961, along came Jonathan weighing in at 10 pounds and 2 ounces. What a big boy! It was not an easy birth and I do remember it well. But it was well worth it. We had expected his grand entrance about 6 weeks earlier so that would have something to do with his being such a big baby. He was born during a bad winter when we had lots of snow and snowstorms. I know Dad went down to see Barney Smith who was in charge of the county roads, just in case Jonathan decided to come during one of those storms when roads were impassable for an ordinary car. As it turned out we did not need to call on Barney because Jonathan came at a time when we were able to get to the hospital with our own car. I don't remember who took care of you three kids when he was born. I am sure you were at home with someone coming in to care for you. – probably Aunt Mabel. Being such a big baby he was easy to take care of. When he got old enough to eat at the table with the rest of the family I remember how he would usually take a nap on his chair after supper by drawing his knees up under him and lie down on the chair. He would usually go to sleep for a short while. I don't know if he still feels like sleeping after a meal or not but it is not a bad habit. Also when Dad would give him a haircut he got so relaxed and would fall asleep before the haircut was finished. It's nice to be so relaxed. By the time Jonathan was born I sort of had built-in baby sitters. Sarah was nine years old by then and loved taking care of babies. Not only did she take care of her own little brother, she also was known to help out other mothers by pushing their babies in a large baby buggy around the little town of Scarville.

Dad was diagnosed with sarcoidosis shortly after Jonathan was born in 1961. He had been experiencing severe coughing spells for some time. Even though he made numerous trips to the doctor to discover the cause of all the coughing, it was the Red Cross Mobile Unit that came to Scarville and took chest X-rays of the people who had signed up which finally got to the bottom of it. I received a card in the mail saying my chest was OK but Dad's never came. A short time later I was at home when a call came from our rather worried family doctor, Dr. Nesheim in Emmons, Minnesota. He had received a report from the Red Cross that Dad needed to come in immediately. Dad happened to be out golfing. Since I didn't have a car I walked down to Harry's and borrowed his car and drove to the Lake Mills Golf Course to give Dad the news that he needed to get in to the doctor. In a few days he was sent down to the Mayo Clinic where he was diagnosed with sarcoidosis. It required minor surgery of the lymph node to make the diagnosis. I remember having a room about a block from the hospital, and as you can imagine I was pretty worried. The family is all aware of what a hard time that was, but we had hopes that he could be cured. Unfortunately it had gone on too long. However, he learned to live with it and thanks to the wonderful Dr. Arthur M. Olsen at the Mayo Clinic he was able to accomplish much while carrying this handicap. We all helped in many ways to share the burden.

Dad's first trip to Arizona
When Jonathan was only about two years old Dad took a trip to Arizona because of his health. He had hoped the drier air might be of benefit to him. Two men from the Scarville congregation drove out with him, John Knutson and Erik Brudvig; Dad did the driving. I don't remember how long they were there before I joined Dad by taking the

train from Albert Lea to Phoenix. I remember at one of
the whist parties the Scarville congregation always had they
gave me the lunch offering and I used it to buy my train
ticket. Dad was so happy that I could join him for a few
days. I rode back to Scarville with all of them, of course,
in Erik's car. I don't believe the trip had the desired effect
on Dad's health but it was worth a try. However, he was
able to keep on as pastor for many years. Jonathan stayed
with Orpha and Les Storby while we were gone. He loved
Orpha so much – she was always a special friend to our
family. We couldn't have gotten along without her. I still
remember the surprised look on Jon's face when I picked
him up after we got home. Mabel had come down to stay
with you other children. She was a great donut baker and
Teddy especially loved Aunt Mabel's donuts. It was good
to get home again.

August 1, 1965, was a great day – Joel was born! It was
on a Sunday and Dad had to go to Thornton, Iowa, for a
young people's meeting of some sort. Earlier on that day
it was beginning to look as though I would be taking a trip
to the hospital. Mabel was staying with us at the time.
Probably since we were expecting Joel to make his grand
entrance into the world and we would need someone to
take care of the home fires and help Dad out while I was in
the hospital. It was a good thing that Mabel was there because she is the one who had to drive me to the hospital. I
remember that afternoon well since Lena and Emma Sande
came over to visit. I am sure we had coffee and they stayed
quite awhile. We were beginning to wonder when they
would be leaving since the time was coming when I needed
to go to the hospital but not before I had some sweet corn

for a light supper. I wasn't going to leave without having my sweet corn. It was the first of the season. I probably sat around there too long before leaving for the hospital. Mabel and I had quite a wild ride. I know Emma and Lena were so surprised the next day to find out Joel was born a few hours after they were there. Dad had been notified of our situation at home and he came barreling into the hospital in time – but not too much time. Teddy who was with him down at Thornton said Dad had passed two cars at a time to make it home. He probably had to go by way of Scarville first to leave Teddy there before going on to the hospital. Everything went fine and we had Joel. In those days we didn't know ahead of time whether it was a girl or boy and I think it is just as well to keep the surprise until the exact moment of arrival. I remember when I got home from the hospital with Joel, our neighbors, the twin ladies, Evelyn Escherich and Elaine Albertson were outside waiting and hurried over to see the newborn. When Jonathan saw Joel he said, *"Mom, they gave us a baby with no teeth!"* Teddy hurried down to Reiso's store and bought him a little toy baseball mitt and bat to chew on. Bringing home a new baby was always a big thrill in the family, in the neighborhood, and the two congregations. By this time I had lots of babysitters right in the family.

Now what did Joel do that I can write about? He was really cute! (*I need to insert one of Clair's clever remarks here because it comes to mind and I don't want to forget it.*) *When Joel, Deanna, and Clair stay overnight Clair sleeps on a blowup mattress right next to my bed. I was pointing to the picture on my bedroom wall that has all five children's early pictures on it and I happened to say to Clair how cute her Daddy was. She*

The Aaberg Family in the early 1960s
Theodore, Sarah, Teddy, Melvina
Baby Jonathan, & Marie

The Aaberg Family in the late 1960s
Teddy, Marie, Sarah
Melvina, Jonathan, Joel & Theodore

said, "Was he the cutest little kid in the whole wide world?" And I said, "Yes, he was." I'll never forget that. The photographer in Forest City thought so, too. When we had our family picture taken he took a picture of Joel and had an enlargement made of it which he kept in the window of his studio for quite a while. I always wished we could have bought it. Joel loved little cars to ride in and although we didn't have one, he got to use one of the neighbor's little boy's car occasionally. When we moved to Norseland when he was three years old we made arrangements for a friend of ours at Norseland, Lois Annexstad, to purchase a little car for him which was waiting in the Norseland garage upon our arrival. That was a big hit and a nice thing for Dad to think of.

We took a trip out to Boston in July of 1967. *(Paul Madson says it must have been in '67 since he had just come to Boston in '66.)* Joel was only a little under two years old at that time and Sarah remembers he was quite a handful ☺. I don't know what car we had at that time but when I find some photos I will be able to tell. Also the date will probably be on the picture so I will find that out, too – but I am sure Paul is right. As I was looking in a dresser drawer in Marie's bedroom for some mementos that I kept there, I found a notebook Marie had kept about our trip to Boston. I will quote from that here:

> *We started out on our trip with our odometer at _____.*
> *At about 10:30 we stopped at a place around Roch-*
> *ester. After dinner we continued our trip. Later that*
> *afternoon we went to a town name Baraboo, Wiscon-*
> *sin, famous for its circuses. In this town we stopped at*

a museum called the World Circus Museum. We got in at 1/2 price here with our Mobil Tickets. Just by chance we got there when they had just started their one ring circus. We hurried to the hippodrome. Just as we were walking in a clown came right in behind my brother Jonathan and kept walking to our seats like one of our family. With everybody there looking at him to see what his reaction would be. But Jonny just sat there with a sober face looking straight ahead. Then all of a sudden the clown jabbed Jonny in the ribs and ran off into the ring.

The one person in our family who was really fascinated was my brother Joel. He got such a thrill from this one act where they had these poodles jump on the backs of horses. When the act was over and the acrobatic act was done, Joel was yelling, "horsy come back."

After the circus was over we went to tour the grounds where we saw some posters from the circus and some museums.

Dad was always good at getting the children to write a diary about our trips. He bought each one – that is the older ones, a notebook for this very purpose. Marie kept a pretty good diary from which I took my information. We stopped at John and Brenda's in Chicago for a couple of nights on the way. This would have come sometime after the Baraboo Circus stop. While there we visited the Art Institute which makes me think Uncle Joe must have been accompanying us for that bit of site seeing - the artist that he was.

On July 7th we reached Boston and got our things settled into Paul's house as Marie notes in her diary. During the days that we were there we made a trip to Cape Code where we visited Christian Moldstad. I remember Paul and Dad had to help him up from the ocean beach since the sand was so deep that it made walking difficult for an old man, especially when his shoes were filled with sand. Teddy remembers that John Moldstad, his wife Gudrun and John Jr., Donnie, and Lois were also at the cape. That accounts for caricatures of the three children in Marie's notebook. Could it have been Donnie's artwork? No, it wasn't. ☺. We definitely visited many historical sites which are so important to our history: To name a few: Paul Revere's home, Faneuil Hall, Lexington and Concord, Old Ironsides, Old North Church, King's Chapel, First Meeting House, Plymouth Rock, Mayflower Ship, and Bunker Hill Monument where we climbed up all 394 steps. Dad stayed below with 2 year old Joel. <u>Now</u> he could make it ☺.

One other very important thing to remember was that Jonathan spotted $5 right behind our car when we were coming back to it after one of our site-seeing tours. I don't know who decided this but we all got an ice cream treat out of it. On talking with Jon the other day and wondering who decided that, he said, *"I don't remember having any objection."*

This story Marie found in her scrapbook relates to the incident:

> *On our way down to Plymouth Rock we drove into a busy street in town where we thought we were really lucky to see this one empty parking spot. But just as we*

were going to get out of the car we saw a big swarm of
bees. So then we were going to find another parking
space. Right then we saw a lady come, walking down
the sidewalk right into the bees. Then one got down
her back and she started to wiggle around trying to get
the bee out. Then another lady came along and had
to unzip the lady's dress and help her get the bee out.
And it was just luck that the bees were there because
in the next parking spot Jonny found 5 one dollar bills
curled up.

I need to add that we would never have been able to take a
trip like that without the generosity of Paul Madson who
was pastor in Boston (Cambridge) at the time. He let us
make our home with him in the parsonage during that
time. Boston is not an easy town to find your way around
and as we were in the general area of the parsonage fairly
late at night, we just couldn't find it without giving Paul a
call and having him come down and direct us. He was a
great tour guide taking time to show us the sights of Boston. I need to add that Dad offered to preach for Paul the
Sunday we were there and I am sure Paul appreciated the
day off.

Childhood diseases
I put this in here because we had our share of them while
in Scarville. The strange thing is that I, the mother, came
down with the mumps and exposed my children to it. The
three oldest all got it but I don't think that Joel and Jonathan were born yet then. If I am not mistaken they later
got a vaccine to protect them from it. We had all been up
at Oklee, Minnesota, where Bill Petersen was pastor and

we stayed at the parsonage there for a long weekend while Dad was, I am sure, preaching for mission festival or some such thing. I don't know if I got exposed to mumps there or someplace else, but there was no question that I had the mumps. Dear Aunt Mabel came down again and took care of us. We have photos of the children, especially Marie, to prove that they did have the mumps. We got through it all. They also all had chicken pox, I believe. But Joel didn't get chicken pox until we lived in Mankato. Dad and I had gone on a long weekend trip to northern Minnesota to visit some cemeteries where Dad's relatives were buried. I don't know if it was on his mother's or father's side. Sarah and Marie were home taking care of Joel.

Then another thing was the red measles. That can be a really serious disease, and I remember one Sunday afternoon lying in a bedroom upstairs in the Scarville parsonage with all of the children. I had the shades pulled because we needed to keep them out of the bright light to protect their eyes. They were coughing and coughing. I am pretty sure that Dad was in Story City, Iowa, preaching since that was a once a month charge that he had. We got through that without any bad residual effects. I was lucky that I had the measles and the chicken pox when I was a child so for those two diseases I was spared and able to take care of my children.

Children's Writings
The other day I came across this story that Teddy had written for a school assignment in English.

One day as I was on my paper route I stopped at the garage to give a paper to them. In the corner was a bum sitting on a kaat (sic). He wore faded blue overalls with blood shot eyes, and he only had one tooth so it was hard to understand him. He said in a stuttering voice, "Come here." I went over, and he gave me a dollar to put in missions. I said thank you in a loud voice. Then I knew beneath those clothes lay a heart of gold, because he probably saved one's soul.

Just yesterday I came across **Teddy's Autobiography** in one of Dad's boxes downstairs. I was so excited to find it and am quoting it here:

The Life of Ted Aaberg, Jr.

Written by Ted Aaberg, Jr.

On December 16, 1952, Rev. and Mrs. Theodore Aaberg had their 1ˢᵗ baby of five. It was a boy named after his father, Rev. Theodore Aaberg. This boy was me. I was baptized the day I was born in the hospital by my father. Two weeks later in church I had part of a service where my sponsors would be there. My sponsors were my Grandma, Grandpa, Milly Johnson, Joe Aaberg and Rev. and Mrs. Paul Petersen.

A year later on October 8, 1953, I got a sister named Sarah Aaberg. The next year I got another sister on November 23, 1954, named Marie Aaberg.

In the summer of 1955 we went out West to visit my Grandma and cousins at the age of Teddy 3, Sarah 2, Marie 1.

At then age of 6 I started school which I didn't like at all at first. The first two weeks I was in kindergarten. Then I passed into first grade which was a lot better.

When I was in second grade we went on a trip to Colorado and the Black Hills where my Great Uncle Melvin Johnson lives.

In the year 1961 I got a brother named Jonathan Aaberg.

The biggest thrill in my life has happened 7 times, but the first time especially. It was a Twin's Game. This will always be one of the biggest thrills in my life.

My most favorite sport is baseball by miles. Then it's basketball. The reason I like baseball is that it takes lots of skill, brains, and experience. My favorite positions are 3rd, 1st, right field.

The reason I like basketball is because of the fast action, ability to use skill and quick thinking, and because you can't be clumsy.

In 1964 I went to Summer Camp where I had lots of fun.

On May 26, 1966 I graduated from Grade School from Scarville Lutheran School.

On June 5, 1966 I was confirmed in the Center Lutheran Church with a class of 4 boys, Dale Olsen, David Storby, Jack Cox, Teddy Aaberg.

FUTURE

Next year I plan to go to high school at Bethany Lutheran High School. Then I plan to go to college there too for two years. Then I plan to go to either Mankato State or Minnesota University, in Minneapolis. I also plan to play baseball in these places.

Then I hope I will be able to get a contract with some Major League team. This I hope very much that this will come true. If not I will be something in sports like a commentator or a coach.

Ted Aaberg Jr.

Written June 6-8, 1966

Jonathan wrote this one about the storekeeper, Sievert Reiso, in Scarville, Iowa. I think it's a gem.

The old store keeper was really one of a kind. He was a charming old man. It was very easy to talk with him. He never seemed to become bored by your stories, yet he was very wise with his money. He was one of the most generous men I have known. He was very fond of children as shown by the way in which he kept the price of his candy. As far as possible even to the point of making no profit on some. He always kept his store extremely neat, but he did not mind at all if we children played with some of the toys in the display shelf. He liked to keep busy and probably could have lived quite well without his store. But by running his store he kept himself busy. He had quite enough money and by running his store he provided an important link in the community, which affected all of our lives.

Jonathan Aaberg,

Sarah's Autobiography.

Chapter I

Birth and Ancestors

I was born on October 8, 1953, at Naeve Hospital in Albert Lea, Minnesota. My full name is Sarah Ann Aaberg. I was born on my parents' second wedding anniversary. My parents' names are Theodore and Melvina Aaberg. My mother's maiden name is Olson. All my ancestors on both sides are Norwegian.

I was baptized on November 8, 1953, at Scarville Evangelical Lutheran Church in Scarville, Iowa. My sponsors are Mr. and Mrs. Carl Annexstad and Clarence and Hilma Dale.

There are five children in my family. I have three brothers and one sister. My brothers' names are Theodore Edward (14 years), Jonathan Daniel (6 years), and Joel Christian (one year). My sister's name is Ma-

rie Elizabeth (12 years). I am 13 years old and the second oldest child in my family.

Most of my relatives on my father's side live far away. The West Coast is where a lot of them live. My mother's relatives live mostly in central Minnesota near Tracy, Minnesota. Some also live on the West Coast.

Chapter II

Early Life

Before I started school my family and I took several trips. In the following paragraphs I will tell about them.

The first long trip my family and I took was to Tacoma, Washington. I was two years old and Teddy was three years old. Marie, the youngest of all, was only one year old. I don't remember this trip at all because I was so young. I know we went up on Mount Rainer. We've got pictures of it. During this trip we visited many relatives. That was the first time my Grandmother saw me. We stayed in Washington for quite awhile because I have many aunts, uncles, cousins and other relatives who live there. Later we went to California to visit my uncle Marvin and his family. The first time I saw mountains was on this trip.

On our way out west we stopped at the Black Hills in South Dakota. Here we saw Mt. Rushmore, the Needles Eye, and other interesting sites. At the Needles Eye we saw an old man sitting by the road who sold colorful stones. We bought different varieties of stones to take home.

In 1959 my family and I took a trip to Colorado. About all I remember on this trip is that Teddy, Marie and I each had a trampoline to use at the motel where we stayed. In Colorado we saw the Garden of the Gods, Pikes Peak, and a very large zoo which is one of the largest in the country. On this trip I was a little older but I still don't remember very much.

We've also made many short trips to Tracy, Minnesota, where my Grandfather and many other relatives live. We used to go up one day and stay overnight, but now we make a round trip in one day. My Grandpa would be so glad to see us. The first thing he did was to lift all of us children to see how heavy we had gotten since the last time we came. He would always put up a swing for us when we came. He did this until he got to be about eighty years old. We children didn't have too much to do when we went there, but he did have a very nice tool bench which we got to use occasionally. I guess he was kind of particular about his tools. By his house there was a grove of trees where there was an old stove. Marie and I used to play house in there. It was a lot of fun. Mom would take us uptown one day while we were there. Grandpa would say we could buy what we wanted. We would usually go and visit our relatives who live close by. A few years ago he had a stroke, and now he stays in the nursing home in Tracy. We usually go up there during our school vacations. He always likes to have us come and visit him.

I have lived in the town of Scarville all my life. It is a very small town with a population of less than a hundred people. The business places include the grocery stores, an elevator, and a café. There are several larger towns nearby. There has not been too many playmates my age in Scarville. I've played with Linda and Diane Smith, Ginger Meyer, and several others that have moved away.

Chapter III

School Life

I started school the first day the school started. The year was the fall of 1958. I have gone to Scarville Lutheran School since I was in kindergarten. There were ten pupils enrolled when the school started. The one room school is in the church.

During my years at school we have presented two operettas, "Hansel and Gretel" was put on when I was in first grade. I was in sixth grade when "The Cowboy on the Moon" was presented.

The school paper, "The Scarville Slate," has been put out about three times a year. I have been on the staff sometimes.

I have participated in the school programs which take place every few months. These programs are called "School Friends." At the end of my eighth grade year I shall graduate from grade school. Graduation is on May 26, 1967. The members of the graduating class will include myself. My class has had up to five members.

During grade school I went on several field trips. We went to such places as a 7up company in Mankato, and on this trip we visited a fire and police station. One year we took a very interesting trip to the Mayo Clinic in Rochester, Minnesota. We went to St. Paul, Minn. where we visited the Como Park Zoo. On one of our trips we stopped and toured the Graphic Publishing Company in Lake Mills, Iowa. On this trip we also visited a zoo in Mason City, Iowa. Every other year we go to Saude and Jerico Christian Day Schools and play a softball game. The years we didn't go to their schools they came to ours.

I've had five teachers during my grade school years. For kindergarten and first grade La Vonne Johnson was my teacher. Helen Kuehl was my teacher for second grade. Adela Halverson was my teacher for third, fourth, and fifth grade. My teacher for sixth grade was Rosella Iverson. Diane Natvig has been my teacher for seventh and eighth grade.

I've had various jobs during my school life. The paper route has been my job during my eighth grade year. I've also done a lot of baby-sitting lately. Last summer my girlfriend and I had the job of cleaning the park facilities. I've had jobs of raking and mowing for people in town.

In the summer of 1964 I went to summer camp. It took place at Squaw Point Resort near Onamia, Min-

nesota. *That was the only time I had gone to summer camp.*

During the summers my family and I have taken several vacations to resorts. Several summers we went to Squaw Point Resort. Some other places we went to were Duluth, Minn., Pine River, Minnesota, and a cabin forty miles southwest of Ashland, Wisconsin.

I have many hobbies. One of my favorite ones is baking. On Saturdays I usually like to bake several things. One of the most favorite things I like to bake is a Swedish tea ring. Some of my other hobbies are knitting, sewing, reading, and playing the piano.

When I was in my early grades at school I started taking piano lessons from my mother. When I was in eighth grade I took lessons from another lady.

At home I help with many jobs. Among them are washing dishes, ironing, spring and fall house cleaning, watching my little brothers, as well as my hobby of baking.

On July 4, 1977, I got confirmed at Scarville Evangelical Lutheran Church. Karen and Daniel Faugstad, Dennis Olson, and myself are in the class.

Future Life

I am looking forward to going to Bethany Lutheran High School this fall. In the future I would like to become a Christian Day School Teacher. My reason is that I have gone to a Christian Day School, and I would like to help other children as much as this school has helped me.

Sarah Aaberg

Children's playmates in Scarville

Earlier I mentioned the children's friends, but will elaborate a little more on it here. Teddy's very best friend was Danny Sabo. They had a great time playing baseball up at the Scarville ball diamond right in the corner of town and only a couple of blocks from our house. Sometimes you could hear them pretending they were players in a big league and one of them would be announcing the plays like the "big guys" do. Teddy had the game, "All Star Baseball" which they played a lot. We still have that game and it shows wear but I think it could still be used. I know one time Dad and Mr. Sabo took the boys up to a Twins game. That was really a very special day for them. Dan Sabo liked some of the musical records we had. I remember he thought it was so great that we had "*The Brandenburg Concerto*" by Bach. (This was a Christmas gift to our family from Paul Madson.) So it wasn't only baseball Dan was into at an early age. When he grew up he became a concert pianist. Teddy came back from Boston for one of his performances in Minneapolis. It was probably the first they had seen each other since we moved away from Scarville. It was fun seeing the two of them together after so many years – so many things to talk about. And Teddy with his all his degrees and accomplishments – the two young Scarville boys have done well.

Sarah's playmates were often Linda and Diane Smith. They lived right across the park from the parsonage. They liked taking care of the other little kids around town – especially the babies. I think they did some baking together and played with dolls, too. I remember the Fourth of July celebrations in Scarville. The town went all out for this, and our parsonage was right along Main Street. One year we all got together down in the fire station and made paper flowers for a float, "*The Old Woman Who lived in a Shoe.*" All of the little girls in town were dressed up really cute and rode on it. I don't remember if any of the boys were on the float. We always looked forward to the Fourth of July. There was a picnic in the park for everyone at noon. I believe they had hotdogs and maybe hamburgers and we each must have had to bring something for sort of a potluck. The town had a meeting house where the Booster Club met and made plans for the big Scarville outings. It's nice that a small town could do something like this, and I believe it still does. I can remember one year a man walked in the parade on huge stilts. That really impressed me. Dad and I tried to find things for all the children to do so they could be in the parade when they were old enough. I think one year Marie and another little girl led a little lamb in the parade. Sometimes the kids would just ride their tricycle which would be decorated somehow.

Marie often liked playing with the boys and her best friend was Greg Wuerflien. They spent a lot of time together. Greg lived in a trailer house with his family which stood right next to his Grandma Minnie Wuerflien's house. That was right across the road from our house. Greg's mother,

Blanche, was my very best friend in Scarville. We spent a lot of time visiting back and forth. I liked her a lot. Marie also spent quite a bit of time playing with Teddy and Dan Sabo. She had an old black suitcase which she kept under her bed for storing things she would not part with. To this day Marie keeps quite a collection of things. Sometimes on Sunday afternoons when Veryl Meyer's grocery store was closed, he would let his daughter Ginger and Sarah and Marie come in and play store. They had fun loading up carts and even got to use the cash register. Of course our children always enjoyed their special friendship with Lois and Steven Olson who lived right outside of town across the tracks.

Our Garden on the Church Property
We had a garden over on the church property and also a small one at home. We raised vegetables – green beans, cucumbers, tomatoes, peas, etc. I did a lot of canning in those days. One day I was canning green beans with a pressure cooker and as I had just removed the jars from the cooker they started to ping as they do when cooling off. There was an old Pastor Ingebritson and his wife visiting, (she was a nervous sort of person) and jumped every time she heard the ping. We often got vegetables from members of the congregation. Dad was a good gardener and I think enjoyed it more than I did. We also canned apples and bought crates of peaches to can. I never really enjoyed the canning part, but it was fun to see the finished product pile up on the shelves.

Dad was pastor in Scarville for 19 years and I lived there for 17 years since he was there for two years before we were married. That was a long time for a pastor to be in one place but we loved it there. We had a beautiful home and two wonderful congregations and despite getting a small salary we never lacked for food. When we celebrated our 10th anniversary at the Scarville church we received a large freezer which was a very big gift. We also got food to put into it. Knowing we had a place for meat they were quick to supply things for us.

Dad was managing editor of the <u>Lutheran Sentinel</u> for some years and was also on the Board of Regents of Bethany College as well as the Doctrine Committee. These were two big committees of the synod's structure of which he was a member.

Dad did a lot of traveling to Winkels (the circuit pastors' monthly meetings) and to spring and fall circuit meetings, as well as to the meetings of the important Synod committees he was on. Usually I went along to the spring and fall circuit meetings and brought you children along – fortified with books, small toys, and a few snacks to keep you quiet during the meetings. I always looked forward to those meetings. It was a nice outing for me when I could get together with other pastors' wives. Hazel Newgard always came to those with her family. I think those are more or less a thing of the past these days as far as women coming with their little children. We also had an annual picnic with the pastors of the circuit and their families. We met in different parks and that, too, was always fun. Dad probably was their chief hamburger griller.

For some years I was the organist at Center congregation. I know in that congregation there were a couple of families where the husbands continued the old tradition of the men sitting on one side of the church and their wives on the other. The Palmer and Clarence Olson families honored that tradition. The organ was an old pump organ where someone had rigged up an old vacuum cleaner motor to make the peddles go. That saved me a lot of energy. Once in awhile I substituted as organist in Scarville but not too often.

Dad was elected president of the ELS at its June convention in 1962. The following is taken from Muehlenhardt's M. Div (A brief biography of President Theodore A. Aaberg)

> *The 1962 ELS Convention was huge in Aaberg's life. Not only did he deliver the Convention Essay, but the Doctrine Committee's report was a major part of the Convention business and Aaberg was elected president of the Synod and Chairman of the Board of Trustees. Aaberg was, and remains, the youngest man to have held the office of Synod President in the history of the ELS. (p. 38)*

> *The combination of workload and Sarcoidosis was now becoming too much for him. Pastor Aaberg's health finally forced him to resign the presidency of the Synod, effective October 14, 1963. (p. 42)*

Even after that he was able to write one of the most (if not **the** most) popular Evangelical Lutheran Synod histories, "A City Set On A Hill." The book was published just before we moved to Norseland. Also the 50th anniversaries for both Scarville and Center congregations were held just prior to our move to Norseland. There was a lot of work for Dad to do by way of organizing those anniversaries, as well as supervising the building addition to the Scarville church. I believe it was a good time to move. We had wonderful parties in both churches before we left.

The town's people also had a party for us. Following is the nice letter Dad wrote to those people before we left.

Scarville, Iowa,

July 16, 1968

Dear Friends:

The picnic gathering of townsfolk last Friday evening, arranged by the Scarville Boosters' Club, was a distinct honor to us and one which we will long remember and cherish. We want to express our sincere thanks to one and all for the social gathering, the good wishes, the cards, and gifts of money.

We pray in the fourth petition of the Lord's Prayer for "Daily bread," and as Luther explains in the Small Catechism, this includes: ". . . true friends, good neighbors and the like." For many years the Lord has answered this portion of that petition to us through the people of Scarville.

Scarville has been our town for nineteen years, and it has been a good town; a town of which we have been, and continue to be, proud. In leaving now we say with humility and gratitude: Thank you, and God bless you!

Sincerely,
Theodore and Melvina,
Theodore Jr., Sarah, Marie, Jonathan, and Joel

The Move to Norseland

I am glad to get to this point. *"Leaving Scarville is heart-rending."* That's what Grandma Aaberg said. It was heart-rending to think of us leaving Scarville, to leave a place where our family had lived for so long and made so many friends. All the children were born while we lived in Scarville. Dad had such an outstanding reputation as a good pastor as well as being a strong supporter of Christian education, that he was sought after by several other congregations in the Synod as can be shown by all the calls he had received and turned down. Since I have been recently working on entering some of Dad's files over in the ELS Archives I came across a file listing the following calls: New Richland Congregation, Thornton, IA; Koshkonong near Madison, WI; Saude and Jerico, Iowa; Mayville, ND; East Grand Forks, MN; St. Paul's Lutheran Church, Chicago; and River Heights, Mason City, IA. If I remember correctly I didn't want to move at any of those times. I am sure one reason we stayed so long in Scarville was because of the Christian Day School which Dad was instrumental in reopening after it had been closed for many years due to the lack of pupils. With our young family and the Faugstads and Olsons, as well as others, the time was ripe for starting it up again.[1]

Then along came the Call to the Norseland/Norwegian Grove Parish in 1968. I was kind of excited when that Call came having taught at Norseland Christian Day School for three years right out of college. After careful deliberation and prayer, Dad decided to accept it. Even though there was a certain sadness about leaving the congregations, the people, and the school, there was excitement, too. There was something special about Norseland. We got busy and cleaned out the attic, hauled stuff to the dump, and packed and packed. I know Orpha came to help us, good friend that she was. They had a farewell party for us in the Scarville Church basement. If I remember correctly they ordered Kentucky Fried Chicken from Albert Lea. I am sure Center had a party, too, and I am sure it was fantastic but I don't remember it exactly. I do remember one thing: Kay Anderson grabbed me and gave me a hug as we were walking down the steps of the church and then she said, *Oh, I shouldn't have done that."* I loved getting a hug from her. In those days hugs weren't given out as freely as they are today. It must have meant a lot to me since I still remember it 40 years later, especially since I don't remember anything else about the party. Nowadays I have hugged so many people and gotten a lot in response. I am not that shy, skinny, little Norwegian girl anymore.

---

1   While we lived in Scarville Teddy and Sarah began attending Bethany Lutheran High School – Teddy in 1966 and Sarah in 1967.

Here I want to quote Dad's article in the very last PARISH BULLETIN for Scarville – Center Lutheran Parish, dated August, 1968.

FAREWELL

This week your pastor concludes his ministry in your midst which began 19 years ago, back in July, 1949. In taking leave of the parish, he, together with Mrs. Aaberg and the children, Teddy, Sarah, Marie, Jonathan, and Joel, all express their sincere thanks for the many kindnesses shown them over the years, and also now at their departure. The farewell parties, the good wishes, the gifts, and the help in getting ready to move—all is appreciated very much. May the Lord bless one and all.

Our years and work here were not unlike those which God's people have experienced from the early days of the world, namely, joy and sorrow, sorrow and joy. But over every day has stood the faithfulness and love of God. "And of his fullness have all we received, and that grace for grace." John 1:16.

That your pastor would have shown greater faithfulness and diligence in his pastoral work is only too true; and this he sincerely regrets. For the Law and the Gospel which was preached and applied, however, he has no regrets, but only the happy confidence that this has not been in vain but has and will continue to bear fruit for there is the promise of God concerning His Word: "It shall accomplish that which I please and it shall prosper in the thing whereto I sent it." Isaiah 55.

May the Lord's richest blessings rest upon each and every member, and may He soon send a pious and faithful pastor!

God be with you all! For Jesus' sake! Amen.

It was close to Joel's 3ʳᵈ birthday, August 1, 1968, when the big truck came for us. This move was hardest on Joel I am sure. He used to cry after the move whenever we drove into the parsonage driveway at Norseland and he realized his hopes were dashed again – we weren't ever going back to Scarville. One time on a trip back there to visit we stepped into the back door of the parsonage, but Joel did not want to go in. I guess he knew it wasn't his home anymore. However we know he learned to love and still does love Norseland.

Getting back to moving day – Lloyd Olson, a member of Norwegian Grove Church, was the truck driver. I believe Harold Rodning from Norseland also came along to help. I think that Conrad Faugstad from Scarville congregation was also on hand to help. We had accumulated quite a bit of stuff those total 19 years. Dad was there two years before we were married and then as the family grew, so did the accumulation of properties. After the truck was loaded we took off in the car. There was nothing left in the Scarville parsonage for us to sleep on. We must have gotten partially unpacked the same day in Norseland and slept there that first night. I believe that Dad was installed on the very next Sunday. I remember that our living room was still full of barrels and boxes when our company came – Gay and Bernetta who also brought along my Aunt Elma. Of course, there was a dinner after the service in the Norseland church basement.

Dad's book A City Set on a Hill had just come off the press and he had several copies on display in the basement of the church the day of his installation. I remember Rachel [Anthony] saying, "*I didn't know you were an author.*" Remember the special breakfast we had in the dining room one morning when Dad presented each of you with a special autographed copy of his book? It was a momentous occasion to celebrate a monumental accomplishment. Sarah remembers that Dad prepared the delicious breakfast for us consisting of those small sausages, eggs and toast, plus orange juice and coffee I am guessing. Don't forget – I typed that whole book twice, mostly on a manual typewriter but finished up on an electric typewriter which Dad rented from someplace in Mason City. I was so used to the manual typewriter that it took awhile to get used to the electric one. I stayed up lots of nights typing. Dad would write a chapter and then I typed the rough draft which he would send on to his review committee. When they sent back their remarks, etc. I typed it again. I still remember the last night I typed the final copy. His review committee consisted of Torald Teigen, Ahlert Strand, and possibly Glenn Reichwald.

After the move Dad was busy getting his library organized. Teddy, being so knowledgeable about organizing libraries, helped him with that. Also Dad had to acquaint himself with the parishioners, the schedules of board meetings, various organizations, etc. Since I had taught there for three years I knew quite a few people there already. Norseland especially was a busy congregation and there was much for the pastor to do. And remember there were also two congregations here – Norseland and Norwegian Grove which were about eight miles apart.

Marie was in 8th grade when we moved and Jonathan was in 2nd at Norseland Christian Day School. Joel being only three when we moved had to wait a few years. The teacher that first year was Mrs. Granke. Teddy was probably a junior at Bethany and Sarah a sophomore. Sarah remembers staying at home that year and riding with Allen Quist to school. I believe Teddy stayed in the dorm since he was playing basketball and soccer and needed to be on campus. Unfortunately we didn't have a second car at that time. In fact there was only one time I can think of when we did have a second car and that was when we bought that old Buick from Allen Quist. Perhaps it was because we needed it for driving to Green Giant when you children worked there summers.

I keep finding interesting writings by you children to incorporate into my Journal. Here I quote Marie's autobiography which she wrote as an 8th grader at Norseland Christian Day School.

Autobiography

Early Life

I was born on November 23, 1954, to Theodore A. Aaberg and Melvina L. Aaberg at Naeve Hospital,

Albert Lea, Minnesota. I was baptized on December 12, 1954. My sponsors were Mr. and Mrs. Arlin Zingg, Ida Aaberg (Mrs. Bernard Callies) and Herman Aaberg. My Father and Mother are both all Norwegian so I am too.

There are seven persons in my family: My father, Theodore A. Aaberg, my mother, Melvina L. Aaberg whose maiden name was Olson, my brother, the oldest of us kids is Theodore Edward Aaberg, 16. The next oldest is my sister, Sarah Ann Aaberg, 15. Then myself, Marie Elizabeth Aaberg, 14; next is Jonathan Daniel Aaberg, 8, and the smallest is Joel Christian Aaberg, 3. Most of my father's relatives live on the West Coast. A few live in Chicago. My mother's relatives live mostly in Central Minnesota around Tracy, with a few on the West Coast. My Grandpa on my mother's side lives in a rest home in Tracy, Minn. He is 90 years old. My Grandma on my father's side lives in Tacoma, Washington. We lived in a small town called Scarville in Iowa. I was the only one my age, but I still had fun.

School Days

I started kindergarten at Scarville Christian Day School in 1960. There was one boy in my class during my kindergarten year, but after that year he moved away. So for the next seven years I had no one in my grade. My teacher in kindergarten was Miss Helen Kuehl. In grades 1 – 3 Miss Adela Halverson was my teacher. Miss Rosella Iverson was my teacher in 4th grade. From grades 5 through 7 I had Miss Diane Natvig, and in the eighth grade, Mrs. Granke. Dur-

ing my years in Christian Day School I have gone on several field trips and we have also played ball with several of the Christian Day Schools.

Vacations

Our family has gone on quite a few vacations. When I was 1 year old our family went on a vacation to the West Coast to visit relatives and go sight seeing. We saw Mt. Rainer and other things that I can't remember since I was young. On the way to Washington we stopped at the Black Hills. When I was just a few years old we also took a trip to Colorado where we saw a lot of beautiful scenery in the Rocky Mountains. On the way home from Colorado we stopped at the Black Hills and saw the Rushmore Memorial. We have also gone to resorts. We went to Squaw Point several times and Red Rambler and more. In 1968 our family took a trip out East to Boston. We saw many interesting things – the Atlantic Ocean, Paul Revere's home, the grave of many famous authors and other people. We also saw the Old North Church, the homes of famous people, Old Ironsides, Valley Forge, and on the way we saw Chicago where we toured the Art Institute. We also saw the home of the Ringling Brother's Circus in Baraboo, Wis.

Jobs

In the year 1967 I got a job delivering papers. This paper route had been in our family seven years. I also did a lot of baby-sitting in Scarville, a lot of lawn raking and also some mowing. Besides this, of course, I had some chores to do around home.

Moving

In the summer of 1968 Dad accepted a call to the Norseland and Norwegian Grove congregations. I did not want to move. I had lived in Scarville all my life, but we moved on August 2, 1968. This was the day after Joel's birthday. Shortly before we moved the town had a picnic for us and we were invited out for a lot of dinners. Also both congregations had farewell parties for us.

Although I didn't like to move, I did meet some real nice friends, Nancy Swenson, Janet Swenson and Elaine Annexstad here. This year is the first year I have had classmates in my grade. They are Janet Swenson, and Elaine Annexstad. This year I am being confirmed. We have gone up in front of the church 4 times for catechization. We will have it 3 or 4 more times. I will be confirmed sometime in June. There are 9 in my confirmation class.

Future

In my future I plan to attend Bethany Lutheran High School in Mankato, Minnesota. If Bethany would not stay open next year, I will attend Martin Luther Academy in New Ulm, Minnesota. I plan on becoming either a missionary or a Christian Day School teacher. In the summer I hope to get a job to earn some money for my schooling next year.

Things to remember about Norseland Before I get into too many other things, I want to write a little bit about the beautiful countryside, the wooded area around Norseland, and the lake – not to forget the Boy Scout Camp. It was a real playground, full of adventures for you children all the years that we were privileged to live there. I know we got some of you skis from the Swedish Kontur so you could take off into the woods after school on snowy evenings. I can still remember seeing Jonathan ski off into the woods behind the school and later on he would come skiing back along the ditch from the other direction.

I don't know if this should be under Joel's paragraph or under Sarah's but decided to put it here. I found it while cleaning out the file in my bedroom yesterday. She had evidently written it for one of her classes at MLA or DMLC.

The Days of a Four-Year Old

My brother Joel, a four-year old, fills his day with many varied activities. The first event on his list is to have breakfast while watching "Captain Kangaroo," and then listen in on his show "Romper Room." He always stands at the TV participating in the "Pledge of Allegiance." He learned this perfectly just from hearing it. Then he loads the bathtub with toys and takes his daily bath. This lasts almost an hour.

After this he begins to notice the quietness around the house. Joel follows my mother around whining as she does her daily tasks, "What is there that's fun to do?"

Joel always has to call his Dad at the church study to tell him dinner is ready. Near the end of the meal he begins his lecture on why he doesn't need a nap because he has so many muscles. His lecture, having been all in vain, he cheers himself up by having a race up the stairs with his Dad. He lies down but seldom falls asleep.

When the rest of the family gets home from school Joel's day goes faster. He fills us in on the latest news from "Captain Kangaroo." Then he tells us that he left some of the cookies for us. Joel also repeats with some variations the things he hears on TV. For example. "I switched to Crest and now I've got fewer teeth!"

By the time supper is ready Joel is anxious to call everyone to come. Joel also always has to get the devotion book, and he reads a story too. This is his favorite: "Timmy went to a baseball game and he broke a window with a baseball bat. Then he went home and told his mother about it and she got mad."

In the evening he is livelier than ever when people are trying to study. He coaxes you to come and watch a TV show. At bedtime he is still going strong and I'm sure he would gladly talk all night if someone would listen.

Not all days are so boring. He loves to visit old people and shake hands with them. On Sunday he has to be sure to shake hands with his Dad on the way out of the church service in Norseland or his whole day is a failure.

I also remember Joel taking the most difficult route when he went to school by walking on the very top of the high bank of snow which had been made by Teddy Ness when he plowed the parking lot. Joel especially loved his campfires out at Norseland – something that he still enjoys immensely today.

Now I want to write about what a good friend Rachel Anthony has become over the years. One of the first things I learned about Rachel was that we celebrate the same birth date, August 20. I was born 10 years before she was but on that same date which is all-important to Rachel and to me. Occasionally we get together and celebrate our birthdays. The kitchen parsonage was in the process of being remodeled when we came to Norseland. Rachel was the person in charge of that project and worked hard zip stripping the wainscoting on the lower half of the kitchen walls in order to restore them to their former beauty. She also designed the island down the middle part of the kitchen which gave us the long counter area where we ate our meals while the other side housed the stove, refrigerator and cupboards. There was also a new dish cupboard built along one wall which is still in use today but the island has long since been replaced when the kitchen went through another remodeling. I can still remember the first time I met Rachel and that was when she walked up the driveway to the parsonage. I count her as one of my dearest friends and she has also continued to help me in so many ways over the years.

We had to purchase a new electric stove since we did not bring our gas stove from Scarville. There was a church member in Norseland, Teddy Ness, who was an electrician, and since he was on vacation when we arrived, we had to wait quite awhile to get our new stove hooked up. The Trustees did not want to pay the cost of having it hooked up when they could get a man in their own congregation to do it for nothing. We managed. They also put in carpeting for us in the dining room and living room as well as up the staircase in the front of the house. The front staircase has beautiful stained glassed windows – three or four I believe. It was a gorgeous parsonage to live in and I have very special memories of it as you children do, too, I am sure.

I need to put in here that the following year after we moved to Norseland, 1969, Uncle Olaf was taken to his eternal rest. He was 91 years old. It was a sad time – he had taken the place of a father for me since my own father had died many years ago. It was a time full of memories of the years he and Aunt Marie had taken good care of me and my four older brothers. I always looked up to him and respected him.

When we first moved to Norseland Joel noticed the weather vane on top of the church and asked, *"Who shot that arrow up there?"* I guess he thought we were in Indian Territory. Then another time when they were repairing the church someone noticed there was a hole through the round window directly over the altar and Dad questioned whether Joel had done that with his BB gun, but later I know was satisfied that Joel was not guilty.

Ladies Aids: Since there were also two congregations in this parish there were two Ladies Aids to attend and I went to both of them. Dad always had a good devotion for these occasions. Both places had wonderful cooks and the meals and lunches were always good. I know in Norwegian Grove they had a regular supper for their meetings consisting of salads and sandwiches plus a dessert or in winter a hotdish and salads plus a dessert. That's where we had the creamed chicken hot dish that got to be such a favorite for our family. They also had an annual bake/craft sale which went over big in the community.

Norseland ladies continue to be noted for their finesse in organizing celebrations for many occasions. A group of ladies always came to the parsonage to celebrate the pastor's wife's birthday. Many of the older ladies also got celebrated when they had a birthday of note. While many church Ladies Aids have fizzled out – not so with Norseland. Some well-known and fondly remembered yearly projects included the all-famous *Lutefisk Dinner*, and the *Sytende Mae Smorgasbord*. There was always a *Christmas Brunch* after the Children's Christmas Program and often an *Easter Breakfast*. The women of the congregation put a lot of effort into these celebrations, especially the Lutefisk Supper and the 17th of May Smorgasbord but it is a way of bringing the community in to enjoy good food and fellowship. I am glad I still live close enough in my old age so that I can attend some of those special events.

The congregations in both places take advantage of celebrating their anniversaries. In 2006 Norwegian Grove celebrated its 125th Anniversary and in 2008 Norseland celebrated its 150th Anniversary – a big anniversary, too much to write about here. I am so proud that our entire family was able return to Norseland, a place we had all lived and

loved so much. It was a great day celebrating three anniversaries: the Norseland Church, the Scandian Grove Church
and the little town of Norseland.

Janitor Work: For most of the years that we were in Norseland (1968-1976) our family was in charge of the janitor
work for the church as well as keeping the grounds mowed.
That included the church, the Christian Day School, the
parsonage and I believe three pretty good-sized ditches. It
was quite a job since we did it all with our two little Lawn
Boy mowers. I can still remember how hard it was to start
them sometimes. Dad took pride in having the church
grounds well kept and I know the members appreciated it.
One nice thing I remember was the men came and raked
the parsonage lawn every spring, and someone had charge
of clearing the parking lot when it snowed. When all of
you children were away from home or busy with school I
did the mowing and cleaning myself. Norseland church
basement, in addition to being used for its own activities
like Saturday Day School, Ladies Aid, and Young People's
Society, Voters' Meetings, etc., was used for Farm Bureau
banquets and the like. This made a lot of extra work setting up tables for certain events, taking them down again
for other things, etc., but not to complain – we enjoyed all
those activities and getting together with the people of the
community was a big part of living in Norseland which we
enjoyed very much. During the Lenten season there was
always coffee served after the services in the church basement. I remember the most memorable one was after the
sixth Lenten service known as "Pie Night," and continues
to be so.

I happened to find this little article Jonathan had written in his notebook which relates to his janitor work. I quote:

It happened one day while I was more or less going about my normal janitorial duties in our church. My brother and I were riding around the storage racks for chairs when suddenly we crashed into another one, and somehow my foot became caught between them. Well, this brought some excitement with my sister trying to cut off the blood supply to my leg while my little brother ran home quite shaken and managed to spit out the message to our mother. After I was rushed into the car my mother nearly ran over my older brother who was trying to tie up the muffler so it wouldn't drag. We raced into town with the muffler hitting the ground with every bump. We finally got to the doctor's office and I was carried in. But when the doctor was finished all I needed were some stitches for a cut.

Teddy reminded me the other day that one time he rode his bike all the way from Mankato to Norseland. I believe he had a Schwinn bike. I also remember one time he surprised us by bringing out a large green Weber grill for us – not on the bike, of course. That was a wonderful gift and we made good use of it for many years. We still had it when we moved to our home on Adams Street. Orville Quist taught Teddy how to drive tractor and hired him to do some fieldwork and other work around the farm. Orville was a kind and wonderful fellow and I know Teddy very much enjoyed his work there and learned a lot from him. Norseland was probably the beginning of some of Teddy's carpentry skills since Orville loaned him some tools which he set up out in our garage. He built a very nice desk which I am enjoying in my computer room since it hasn't made its way out to Somerville yet.

Green Giant: Everyone in Norseland, Norwegian Grove and surrounding areas was familiar with Green Giant. Many of the farmers grew peas and corn for the cannery at LeSueur, and many of the men, ladies and youth of the congregations worked for Green Giant in one capacity or another. Teddy, Sarah and Marie all worked there during the summers – earning money for high school and college. Teddy drove a forklift and stacked canned corn while Sarah and Marie were huskers. They were both able to often earn top bonus by husking 4,000 or more ears of corn per hour. There was a lot of competition amongst the huskers to see who could husk the most ears in an hour. At times Sarah and Marie were the top huskers. When school started in the fall I filled in for the girls thereby keeping their job going and earning more money for their schooling. I worked the night shift and those 12-hour shifts were long, cold nights. Driving those back roads to LeSueur was dark and sometimes scary. Jonathan, I know, detasseled corn for Hubert Anderson – he still occasionally talks about what a great guy Hubert was. Joel and Jonathan both put in some time walking beans and picking rocks at Julian Olsen's.

Busy Schedule
Dad had a busy schedule with two congregations to take care of– preaching twice a Sunday as well as the weekly Lenten services in both congregations, two Ladies Aids, Young People's meetings once a month, confirmation classes, adult instruction meetings, church board meetings (always ending with coffee and treats I might add), and Satur-

day/Sunday School Teachers' meetings. At times when Dad was sick with a bad cold I substituted for him and taught confirmation class and Saturday School. Just the other day I had coffee with Marilyn and Warren Rodning. We were reminiscing about our days at Norseland. Marilyn, who had taught Saturday School, remarked how impressed she was with Dad's knowledge and how much she learned through the meetings he had for the teachers. It makes me feel good to hear things like that. He was always very well prepared. There were often hospital and shut in calls to make. He never shirked on his duty to minister to those who needed him whether it was to teach, comfort or sometimes rebuke them for their lack of attendance in church or whatever it might be.

All this while the children and I (especially me) were worried about how his health was holding up when the workload seemed to pile up. But he usually got through it. Of course there were a few times when he had to have a substitute preacher. I remember shortly before the first Christmas we were there he got pretty sick with the Hong Kong Flu and had to be hospitalized in Rochester. His doctor, Dr. Arthur M. Olsen, who had been his primary physician ever since being diagnosed with sarcoidosis in '61, was always quick to make arrangements for his hospitalization when that became necessary as it did on several occasions. Those were always scary times for him and the family. It was only by the grace of God that we were able to get through those trying times. As it turned out he was able to be up in the pulpit preaching on that Christmas. I don't believe he missed a single Christmas service all the while he was in the parish ministry, and likely never missed a festival service of any kind. I remember many times I tried to get him to stay at home and not push himself so hard but it was his way.

Education: We lived in Norseland from August 1968 until August 1976 and these were important school years for the family. Joel, Jonathan and Marie attended Norseland Christian Day School. Sarah and Teddy attended Bethany High School until it closed in 1969 just as Teddy was going into his senior year, Sarah her junior year, and Marie her freshman year. For the '68-'69 year I know Sarah rode with Prof. Allen Quist to Bethany. Teddy stayed in the dorm that year since he was in both soccer and basketball, and transportation would have been difficult. *I remember hearing that one night while we were having some kind of ladies' meeting at the parsonage, Dad rode with Orville Quist to a basketball game in which Teddy was playing. He must have made a winning basket because I heard the story that he was carried off the court on the shoulders of one of the other players.* I wish I could have been there.

Following the closing of Bethany High School it was necessary for them to finish out their high school years at Martin Luther Academy in New Ulm. Teddy graduated from **MLA in 1970 and Sarah in 1971.** It was a tough adjustment for them to leave Bethany High School and commute to New Ulm. Paul Quist did most of the driving that year except when Teddy got to transport the group with our car one day a week. Both Teddy and Sarah transferred back to Bethany College after finishing their high school in New Ulm. **Teddy graduated from Bethany College in 1972 and Sarah in 1973.** Sarah transferred to New Ulm again to get her teaching degree and graduated from there in **1975 with a Bachelor of Science Degree in Education and a minor in Music.** After graduation she received her first Call to teach at Saude Christian Day School, the same school her father had also taught years earlier.

Marie made it simpler – after graduating from MLA in 1973 she went straight through DMLC and graduated from there in **1977 with a Bachelor of Science Degree in Education and a minor in Science.** Following graduation she followed in her sister's footsteps by accepting the Call she received to teach at Saude Lutheran School. Meanwhile, Sarah had been called to teach at the neighboring parish school, Jerico Lutheran School.

Teddy, who always maintained an interest in library science and research, worked in the Bethany Memorial Library under the direction of the college librarian, Mary Birmingham. After graduating from Bethany he attended MSU from 1972-1974, **graduating from there in 1976 with a degree in Sociology and American History.** He entered Bethany Lutheran Theological Seminary in 1974[2] and **got his Master's Degree in Theology** in 1978 during the years his father was president.

Jonathan completed his education at Norseland Christian Day School in 1975[3] also attended MLA graduat-

2   When he entered Bethany Seminary in 1974 he still had a class(s) to finish at MSU that explains why he graduated in 1976 after completing those classes while attending seminary.

3   He was part of a very good class. His fellow students were Jeanette Anthony, Rolf Annexstad, Barbara and Bruce Swenson. I remember how nice it was to be in church when they were questioned in front of the congregation for confirmation. I doubt they ever missed a question.

ing from there in 1979. He also attended DMLC for 3 years before deciding to take a break in his education. After leaving DMLC, Jonathan worked at the Ben Franklin store in New Ulm for several years with some intermissions. He worked in his Uncle Phil's frame shop in Huntsville, Alabama, and during another period he drove truck with his friend Charlie Baumann. He's always trying different things. In 1987 he enrolled at the University of Minnesota, which I write more about later.

When we moved to Mankato in 1976 Joel was in 5th grade and he completed his grade school education at Mt. Olive Lutheran School in 1979.

Music: Our home never lacked for good music. Sarah was well on her way to becoming a gifted pianist by the time we moved to Norseland. I am quite sure she had begun taking piano lessons from Mrs. Silber by this time. While a freshman at Bethany High School she started taking lessons from Mary Johnson and then progressed to taking lessons from the piano teacher of all teachers, Mrs. Silber. While a student at Dr. Martin Luther College she was able to continue having her as a teacher. Fortunately there was another student there, Ron Besemer, who was also taking lessons from Mrs. Silber. Sarah was able to catch a ride with him for the weekly lessons. Every year a number of pieces were selected by the teacher for each student to perfect and by springtime perform before a judge at the Silber home. I always enjoyed all the practicing on our old piano at home. By the time she became a senior she was ready to give a senior recital in the auditorium at DMLC in front of a large group of people which included many of the music professors at the college. The recital was followed by a reception in her honor. The lunch consisted of some delicious bars and punch. We still call the punch "Recital Punch". I remember Prof. Jaster being there, and how he enjoyed the goodies. Sarah made a beautiful teal blue formal dress for the occasion. Dad and I gave her a sweetheart locket which she wore.

SARAH AABERG
In
Piano Recital
Pupil of Anna John Silber

Dr Martin Luther College
May 18, 1975
Chapel Auditorium
3:30 p.m.

PROGRAM

Bach	Prelude & Fugue in C minor
Beethoven	Sonata Pathetique
	Grave
	Allegro di molto e con brio
	Adagio cantabile
	Allegro
Chopin	Nocturne in E Major
Chopin	Butterfly Etude
Chopin	Duet Etude
Mendelssohn	Rondo Capriccioso
Tauriello	Toccata
Toch	The Juggler

Sarah has used her talent wisely. I remember going with her and her husband Ron to a music store in Milwaukee when she was looking to spend her savings on a Steinway piano. That was a wise decision. She was an excellent piano teacher and for a number of years taught lessons before returning to the classroom as a full-time Christian Day School teacher. I think Mrs. Silber said something like this *"After a few years a car is nothing but a tin can whereas a piano is a wonderful lifetime possession."* That is so true!

———*———

Even though this is jumping ahead four years, spring 1979, I want to add the following at this point.

Along came Jonathan with all this musical talent we never realized was there. Of course at Martin Luther Academy in preparation for becoming a teacher, students were required to take piano lessons. Well – Jonathan got Mrs. Sharon Just for a piano teacher and took off big time! By the time he got to be a senior he was studying under Mrs. Ruth Anderson as the Justs had taken a call to Arizona and Jonathan was chosen to perform the piano solo at the MLA June Night concert which was quite an honor. He played **Toccata by Tauriello** in front of a packed auditorium. Again we were so proud! Dad was not doing very well at this time and even though we made plans for him to attend the concert and graduation service, he was not able do so. I remember he did, however, write Jonathan a note saying he was so sorry not to be there to hear him play **but he hoped to be present to hear his first concert in Carnegie Hall.** Dad could always come up with a fitting, thoughtful remark. As I write this I am almost getting tears in my eyes. By the time he graduated from high school we were living in Mankato so I am getting ahead of myself but will continue on.

On May 15, 1983, Jonathan played in a Piano Recital at the same Martin Luther College Chapel Auditorium while he was a student of Mrs. Ruth Anderson. (Minnesota Music Teacher's Association)

Etude in Db "un Sospiro" by Liszt

There were 44 pupils in this program and Jonathan was the very last one. (the place of honor)

———— * ————

4H The 4H Club was a big thing in Norseland, New Sweden and the surrounding areas. Marie was the only one in our family who joined 4H. She took sewing and baking and raising flowers. I do remember she was not particularly interested in sewing at that time nor did she develop an interest in it later on. I remember she entered some chocolate chip cookies and they turned out very good – and I can safely say they are still her favorite cookie. It probably started way back then in 4H at Norseland. It was a good experience just being together with the other young people in the community. The County Fair was a huge thing out there and it was fun being a part of it. Many of the young people in our congregation who lived on farms entered their animals and participated in many other projects. It was just a big, big thing in Nicollet County.

Nicollet Extension Club This was something for the women of the county and I participated. It was a nice diversion from all my other duties as homemaker and pastor's wife. We had meetings once a month at the homes of the various members. At each meeting we were presented with a topic of something related to homemaking: baking, canning, sewing, cleaning draperies, etc. I also joined a special sewing group led by the county home extension leader who taught us how to tackle some sewing projects which were more difficult than anything I had ever tackled before. We met in the basement of the Nicollet County Bank in St. Peter about once every two weeks or so. When we first started I did not have my own portable sewing machine, but I was able to use an extra one that our leader provided. I remember making a lined plaid cape and skirt outfit. It was quite a deal! I learned how to make bound buttonholes, remember those, and I probably felt pretty classy wearing it. For my next project I made a white cape. I still have this hanging in my basement. That project took some pretty intricate work to get done. Since we had an expert seamstress as our leader we just asked questions until we were able to successfully complete the project.

I also learned to knit sweaters at Norseland and made several with the help of my friend, Evie Anthony, who was and still is a first-class knitter. We met in the homes of club members every week or two, and it was always a lot of fun and very productive when you think of the sweaters that I managed to knit. Now Jonathan is the knitter in the family. When he comes home for Christmas he likes to go down to Mary Lue's Yarn Shop. He has knit caps, mittens and scarves. Nearly everyone in the family has benefited from his knitting. This year he made a cowl for me which is a nice warm woolen piece to wear around the neck. It was certainly a good year to get a cowl with the winter we have had.

During our years in Norseland an addition was built to the church. The lower level made a proper entryway to the basement and the upper level became the pastor's office. Getting a nice office really helped make Dad's work easier especially since they put in an air conditioner for him, something he badly needed to make his breathing easier. Before that time there was no real office at the church, just a small sacristy. And I can still remember the treacherous narrow cement steps that led down to the basement before the new entry was built. Can you just imagine women carrying loads of food down those steps for all the serving that was done over the years? However, I never did hear of any severe casualties.

I can't leave Norseland without telling about the blizzard of the century. So here goes:

The Blizzard of the Century, February 1975.
This was really something to write about and thankfully I have a copy of a letter that I wrote to Marvin and Terry dated February 10, 1975. Since that will be the best account I can give I will copy that letter in its entirety here:

Dear Marvin, Terry & Nancy,

Guess it's about time I wrote you a letter so you don't think we are completely snowed under. Well, we just about are. Suppose you heard about our big blizzard on January, 10, 11, and 12. They call it the worst blizzard of the century. They say there was another terrible one in 1888, but this one beat the bad one we had on Armistice Day in 1940.

I couldn't help but wish Nancy had stayed 6 more days and she would have gotten in on it. That is, after we made it through it OK I wish she could have seen it. For awhile there I didn't know whether I should wish she were here or not. Our electricity was off for 48 hours, but many farmhouses were without heat, light and water for 80 or 90 hours. Our Nicollet County and Blue Earth County. which is the Mankato area, were the most hit. They were going to ask that it be declared a National Disaster Area but I don't know if they got it or not.

Some farm houses got down as low as 18 degrees inside their homes. Many took to the barns to live with the animals. Of course, their animals were pretty ornery since they couldn't milk them as they should without electricity and there was not much water either. A few farms had auxiliary generators and they were lucky. I guess they are terribly expensive, but they say this one storm it paid to have them. I heard the figure (value) of the animals that were lost that were just frozen standing in the fields. I don't know if it was $500,000 or even more than that.

At our house the electricity went off at 6 o'clock just after I had finished preparing supper. That morn-

ing when I went to get the mail at 11 o'clock it was looking pretty stormy and I needed to go to the store for groceries, so Ted said I should go right away. Well, you know how close the Norseland store is and I was plenty glad to get there and get home again. I stocked up on groceries and I even bought milk there instead of going the other direction about a mile down the road to get milk from our member – you know where we got that, Nancy. When I got home Jon and Joel had gone out to play – I noticed their boots and coats were gone. They had gotten off school that day because of the weather. Well, then I got worried about them because the blizzard was coming up fast and I didn't want them out in the woods someplace. I looked in a tunnel they had built in a pile of snow down by the school and they weren't there – I called and called but no answer. Then finally they came from behind the church where they had built another tunnel in a snow bank. I got them in the house so I wouldn't have to worry about them anymore. Ted was sick in bed with a cold. The other kids were all back in school.

In the afternoon it kept storming and they were giving us storm warnings on the radio all the time. Later on that afternoon we went down to church to get the basement ready for Saturday School, Jon, Joel & I. It was kind of hard walking home. Joel & Jon kind of enjoyed the weather and wanted to stay out but I told them they'd better get in.

Our lights had been flickering so I decided to quickly make supper so we could have one hot meal.

Ted drew off about a bathtub half-full of water so we could have water for flushing the stools. Then I filled lots of containers with water and I also filled all the thermoses we had in the house with hot water. I barely got supper ready and the lights went off so we ate in candle light. That night the house wasn't too bad, there wasn't much we could do but sit around in candle light. When it began to cool off too much we went to bed. It was 50 degrees in the house in the morning when we woke up. The wind had really been whipping it up all night and it had snowed an awful lot. All we could see when we looked out the window was a blizzard. Some of the windows had so much snow blown against them that you couldn't even see out.

I got out of bed first that morning and went to check on Jon and Joel. They were sleeping down in the family room in separate beds but during the night they had moved in together and piled all of the blankets on one bed because they were getting pretty cold.

I thought of this little trash burner that had been left here by the former pastor. They used it up in the kitchen and we had it in the basement, but never hooked it up. There were some stove pipes down there but we didn't know if they would work or not. As soon as I opened the basement door I could tell it was quite a bit warmer in the basement than it was upstairs. You know what a basement we've got. Even that was better than being upstairs. We put on lots of clothes when we got dressed that morning. And we kept them on for at least 2 days. We wore our boots, caps, mit-

tens, jackets and a couple of sweaters underneath plus long underwear and then I guess I had nearly every blanket I owned down the basement. That is all that I had at home, the kids have so many at school.

When Ted and the boys came down the basement we got to looking over that little stove. We managed to get those stove pipes to fit with some make-shift tools. We were so glad to get that hooked up. We didn't know whether we could or not. It took quite a bit of doing and most of the morning. When we did finally get it hooked up and saw that it was workable the boys and I dressed up and went out to the garage to hunt for any scraps of wood that we could burn. I guess I shouldn't say get dressed up. We were about as dressed up as we could get. We braved it out to the garage. We had quite a time getting the back door open because so much snow had blown against it and then again getting into the garage. We picked up all the wood we could find that we could burn. When we got that in the boys got busy sawing it up down the basement. They took turns sawing wood and that took quite awhile. Luckily Ted had bought a pretty handy little saw for sawing wood. It's the one that Joel had used when they sawed down all those trees in the woods for that fort, Marvin. If we had only had that wood, but we were not able to venture that far for wood. Ted tended the fire. We had to be careful not to get too hot a fire and run the risk of a chimney fire. I nailed rugs across some of the windows and openings in the basement to make it a little cozier. We got it about 45 degrees down there and that was just a few feet from the stove where we had our thermometer on the table that it was 45 degrees. You don't get much heat from those trash burners, but we were able to cook on them a little. We would stoke it up some to do that. And it was wonderful to have something you could stand next to and get a little heat. We drank a lot of hot coffee and tea. Also we had soup and ham sandwiches and egg sandwiches. We had plenty of food. So we were a lot more fortunate than some who had no heat. They just had candles and tried to do a little heating of water over them, but it didn't work too well.

Jon's bird feeder was pretty well covered with snow and he saw the birds flitting around out there, but Ted wouldn't let him even go that far to clean it off. You can't imagine how a storm like that can get you off your bearings.

When we had used up the wood we found in the garage the boys and Ted tore apart an old table in the basement and sawed that up. We also had about 10# of charcoal left from last summer which we rationed out. We kept pretty busy all day and that was good because it kept our minds occupied and we kept warm that way too. We had to move the card table and chairs down the basement and food – dishes – we even moved the roll-away bed down there and also an old camp cot. We had to make preparations for the night. It got awfully dark quite early on Saturday evening. The blizzard raged all day and there was no sign of life in the outside world. Except we saw a few birds right outside the window. It is a very funny feeling *when you don't know anything that is going on, how everybody is – you keep thinking about these other old people that live around here. There was not any travel of any kind. Not even a snowmobile on Saturday. We didn't even have a transistor radio working. I made about 3 trips out to the garage on Saturday to listen to the radio. I didn't dare start the car but I just turned the ACC on. I didn't care to run it too long as I didn't want to run down the battery. Then I heard how terrible the power failure was in Nicollet County. They were really warning motorists to stay with their cars and not get out and walk. They said snowmobiles would go out in teams as soon as the weather allowed and also helicopters were standing ready to go out and check the highways as soon as the storm subsided. People had a much better chance of staying alive in their cars than leaving them. Lots of people were stranded in their cars.*

Our telephone was out too. Once when I went out to the car to listen to the radio I heard them giving instructions that we should go to a neighbor's house who had heat if you could get there and if you didn't have heat you should call a certain number. I kind of had to laugh about it, because we couldn't get to any neighbor. I didn't know if any of them had heat and our phone was out so we couldn't call a number and if we could no one could come out and do anything about it. But I imagine this did help some people.

The boys slept pretty well during Saturday night. Ted sat up by the stove in the lawn chair all night. He had to throw another stick in the stove about every half-hour. By this time our wood supply was pretty low. We were getting close to tearing up our basement steps that go outside. We had looked over the canned goods shelves and an old cupboard down there, but decided the steps would be the next to go. They would burn better. It was a long-long night. Every so often Ted took the flashlight and looked out a little clear spot on the basement window to see if the bushes outside were still blowing. They were!

It's funny how stories get started. Some heard we burned an old table and the story got out that the Aabergs had to burn their furniture. One lady wondered if I had to burn my nice dining room table. Sunday morning at 7 o'clock we heard a snow plow and what a delightful sound that was. It was still storming quite a bit. The snowplow was followed by an REA truck. The truck stopped and looked a little at the transformer across the road from our house but didn't do anything. I guess they were just checking wires along the road.

When it got a little lighter Jon and I went out in the yard a short distance to try and find some more wood. Joel was sure there was a log down by that fireplace they had outside but we just couldn't find it. We did find a few sticks of wood but nothing much.

Jon had this aquarium in the living room and we worried about it freezing and cracking. Every so often on Saturday night I made the rounds upstairs and stuck my finger in the aquarium to see if it was freezing. It was getting pretty cold but not ice. Anyway on Sunday morning with still no sign of heat coming on we decided to empty it. The fish, of course, had already died. We had also moved some of our plants down in the basement and canned goods from the kitchen down in the basement so they wouldn't freeze.

A little later in the morning I went out again to see if I could find more wood so he wouldn't have to tear up the steps and a couple of guys drove up on snowmobiles. Was I glad to see them. One guy had a mask stocking cap on and other guy had a big fur jacket and hood on. Then with their helmets on I hardly knew who they were. One turned out to be the guy that works at Norseland store and the other in the old Norseland creamery, which now handles fertilizer. They had gotten out and were checking around the country to see how people were. It was so wonderful of them to stop by. They came down in our basement to see our living quarters. Then they went up to the Norseland store and brought us back 60# of charcoal, 4 big Hershey bars, and a gallon of milk. So we didn't have to start on the steps after all. When they found out we didn't have a radio we were going to get one of those later on too. But then in a little while (early that afternoon) a boy who is a sophomore in high school and is also our member, came up on a snowmobile and invited us to his Grandfather's home in Norseland where they had a generator so they had heat. We had to go on the snowmobile, of course, and that presented no problem for the boys and me, but Ted was reluctant to take the chance. He had been having a bad cold all this time and riding a snow-mobile is quite a ride. When you have to sit in back you don't have much room and he wasn't able to ride that way. It just cut off his breathing. He made all the rest of us go first. He wouldn't even have tried it but then we heard from this boy that the wires were down so bad in this area that we may not have lights until next Tuesday. We couldn't see staying down there that much longer. Well, this boy was very accommo-dating. He stood up on his snowmobile and Ted rode on his knees sideways behind with his head down in the collar of his big coat. Even that was hard enough but he made the trip and we got into the home of Ray Anthony's in Norseland. That is the guy that has the shop up there. That was really a blessing to get up there. We didn't pack much for the trip. It was too cold to change clothes and we took our pajamas and Ted's shaving brush and medicine and that was about it. We couldn't carry much on the snowmobile. This boy made four trips to get us all up there. It was won-derful after we got to their house, nice and warm and good food cooking on the stove, a real nice bed to sleep in with an electric blanket and so it was like a winter vacation.

Ted had a conference coming up in Mankato on Tues. & Wed. of the next week and had a paper to write for that but that all was put in the back of our minds. We couldn't do any work but do what we could do to survive. We were kind of worried since Ted had this cold, but otherwise we were warm with all these clothes on and we didn't run out of water and we had plenty to eat so that was a blessing.

But time does hang out, too, down in the base-ment and you don't know how long it will last so when we "abandoned ship" on Sunday afternoon it was a good feeling. The lights came on a few hours after we got to Norseland. I'm sure they came on here at home then, too. When we came home on Monday night our house was nice and warm. We were very fortunate that nothing froze up here. In some homes every ra-diator in the house broke and water ran all over the place. Plumbers were so busy many had to wait a long time for help. Marvin, you know that big house the woman was painting in. Well, they still hadn't moved in and every radiator in that house broke. Now they have to put in a $2,000 new heating system. I don't know if they are still moving out or not. She hasn't been able to come out and work now with no heat. Plumbers are slow in working at it.

Just after we moved home from the Anthony's at Norseland, a lady was stranded out by our house. I guess the Deputy found her and sent her to our house. She was a weird woman. She didn't talk much and when she did it didn't make sense. She was divorced and her four children were in court and she didn't have a home. She lived in her car. I felt sorry for her. She was all in. I wasn't too keen on her staying too long. We had her overnight and she left the next morning. That was Tuesday. The storm was over by then and she had a pretty good night's sleep.

Many people here were worse off than we were. Many had no heat. Their cows went without milking for days. One family slept in their car for 3 nights. That can be dangerous too. One of our members had a small baby that hadn't even been out for baptism yet and then they had to move into the barn with the animals, but that wasn't too warm either so they finally went by tractor to their folks' farm nearby. They didn't have heat either, but it was a newer house and their basement was about 50 degrees. This mother said she had such trouble walking through the snow with her baby, and once she had to lay the baby in the snow bank to pull her own leg out of the snow.

One of our other members took his family across the road to a farmhouse where they had a gas stove in the kitchen. He said he nearly lost his family getting them there. They got so turned around they didn't know where they were going. His wife got so exhausted she refused to go on but they had to pull her along and then one of his little girls went down and couldn't get going on her own again. That couldn't have been much more than a block to walk.

One mother and her son were out snowmobiling and got lost and froze to death near Willmar. The father was on another snowmobile with a 5-year-old daughter and he got separated from his wife and they couldn't find them until the next day. They were found frozen. A sister of one of our members was out snow-mobiling with others on Friday night and she got lost from the group and spent the night in an abandoned pickup. The doors were frozen shut so she sat in the back and somehow she found her way to a farmhouse in the morning. She had spent the whole night in that howling blizzard.

Well, Nancy, you see what you missed out on. Everyone is fine here now. Hope you are all well. Guess I'll have to write other news later.

Love,
Melvina

The blizzard was in January of 1975. Many stories came out of that blizzard. It is something we will always remember – especially Dad, Jonathan, Joel and I. The others in the family remember it in relation to where they were living at the time. Sarah and Marie at school in New Ulm and Teddy in Mankato at Bethany. They, too, have their own stories.

It was while we were at Norseland that Dad picked up the 1929 Model A at an auction in Ivanhoe, Minnesota. It got to be kind of his "Pride and Joy," especially since he was able to drive it to Mankato for the Synod Convention in 1976. He had a lot of fun with that car by driving an older couple from the Norseland parish, Mr. & Mrs. Gunderson, (parents of Irvin Gunderson) around the community. He also took it to the Young People's meeting one evening and gave all of the kids a ride in it, or did he let them drive it around the parking lot? I doubt that. It was nice for him to have it. He also wrote an interesting article on "Antique Cars" which he read on a few occasions. When the Model A lost its spot in our garage it got to be a bit of a problem finding housing for it but for the time being it is housed at a storage shed near Glenville, Minnesota, so I haven't worried about it. The future of the Model A is uncertain. [1]

An Important Call comes
We had been at Norseland for eight years when Dad received the Call to become the first President of Bethany Lutheran Theological Seminary. It was quite a surprise to receive a Call like that. I am thinking that the Board of Regents was meeting at the time and he got the first word of it by telephone. We didn't have a private line out there so many others could have found out when he did. Knowing how the grapevine works at Bethany, I suppose the Board didn't want to wait until he got the message by mail. It gave him a lot to think about and our whole family a lot to think about. I could tell Dad was excited about it. It was exciting but also cause for concern — mainly since for many years his health had always been a major consideration in whatever he or the family did. I never doubted but what he was qualified for the job. He had been a parish pastor and was highly respected as a pastor by the congregations he served and by the synod as a whole. Some of his

1   Now the future of the Model A is no longer uncertain. On October 21, 2010, it was turned over to its new owner, Calvin Nourie, who owns Cal's Towing & Repair, Inc. in Nicollet, MN. Our entire family is very happy that it has found such a fine new home. I expect it will be in good running order this coming spring or summer.

fellow pastors thought it would be a good thing not only for the seminary but also that his health would improve by not having all the duties of a parish pastor. In some respects that probably was so. At least he wouldn't have to be making hospital and shut-in calls. I still remember when Dad accepted the Call he took Joel down by the little campfire site they had down by the garden and told him about it and the upcoming move to Mankato. Soon Joel came into the house and told me what an honor it was for Dad to be President of the Seminary and then he went up to his room and cried. I guess for many of us that says it all when we thought about moving from Norseland to Mankato. Joel wasn't the only one who cried.

In August of 1976 we moved to Mankato. Of course there were the usual farewell parties and that was sad for us and for them. One thing that made it easier was that we were moving to a place we knew so well and had many friends and acquaintances and it was not very far away. We got busy and packed up our stuff and Lloyd Olson from Norwegian Grove moved us. I think it was Harold Rodning who also helped again this time. It was the second move for us from Lloyd Olson. Moving is work, no doubt about it. We moved into the house at 909 Marsh Street which was only a short walk from Bethany College where the Seminary classes were taught for that first year or two. Dad took over his new position on August 1, 1976. He got one of the large rooms on the first floor of Old Main for an office, and I was his part-time secretary. I had a small desk and a typewriter which was in a corner of the room and that was my start as being secretary to the President of the Seminary – a job which I was privileged to hold for 28 years.

Seminary Installation: Theodore A, Aaberg was installed on August 28th of that year. Seminary Professor Milton Otto preached and Synod President Wilhelm Petersen was liturgist. The Rev. Milton Tweit, chairman of the Board of Regents, performed the Rite of Installation. Dad was kind to incorporate some participation from the Norseland congregation: Margaret Annexstad was organist for the service and the Men's Chorus sang. I remember it was a big affair with some of Dad's special friends from the WELS also present.[2] We had them over to our house on Marsh Street for lunch that day. I wonder what I served. I would never undertake anything like that now. I hope we had some good wine to serve with the meal. That would have been awfully nice.

If I remember correctly the classes were pretty good sized those years when Dad was president. Teddy was in his third year at the seminary so was able to have his father for one of his professors. We were so pleased about that and I know he enjoyed that year as well. His year of vicarage was at Our Savior's Lutheran Church in Albert Lea, Minnesota. He was ordained at Our Savior's Lutheran Church on June 11, 1978, just one week before the dedication of the new seminary building. Pastor Richard Newgard preached the sermon and Dad performed the rite of ordination. I remember we were invited to Newgards for lunch following

2   President Oscar J. Naumann of the Wisconsin Ev. Lutheran Synod and Prof. Carl J. Lawrenz, President of Wisconsin Lutheran Seminary were our guests for noon lunch that day.

the service. He graduated at the completion of his vicar-age and received his **Master of Divinity degree from the seminary in June of 1978.**

A new seminary building was in the works so in addition to getting ready for classes Dad was very much involved with the plans and progress of the new structure. It was located on 447 North Division Street right across from the Bethany Campus. It was completed and dedicated on June 18, 1978.

We enjoyed the house at 909 Marsh Street. It had a nice big bathroom on the first floor with a tub and shower. Upstairs there were three bedrooms and also a smaller bathroom and a shower. This was the first time we had a bathroom with a shower. There was a large living room with a whole wall of windows looking out back towards the garden, the alley, and the Catholic baseball field. Now Bethany owns that field. So times change. In fact it changes so much that the house isn't even there anymore. In time Bethany and the Synod wanted to get out of the business of owning and maintaining homes for its employees and began selling them off one by one thereby picking up more land for the expansion of its campus.

It was a new life – no more preaching every Sunday, La-dies Aid meetings, confirmation classes, shut-in calls, etc. The family got to sit by Dad in church. Joel was attending school at Mt. Olive, and Teddy stayed at home that year while he finished the seminary. Jonathan was attending MLA, Marie and Sarah were both teaching school in Iowa at Saude and Jerico respectively.

Duties as President of the Seminary
Dad was busy preparing for his classes at the seminary.
I believe he taught Dogmatics and Church History, two
topics which he was very interested in and well qualified
to teach. I know he was an excellent teacher and well-re-
spected. He took charge of all the affairs of the seminary
including faculty meetings, preparing agendas for and attending Board of Regents meetings, keeping the budget in
check, etc. I remember one of his first tasks was to prepare
a new Seminary Catalog. I think they learned that he was
capable of doing the job he was called to do and able to
run a "rather tight ship." There were many other things
he was called upon to do because of the nature of his office
– preaching at special church festivals and attending quite
a few meetings both in our synod as well as the WELS. As
time permitted he continued to write papers, probably of a
doctrinal nature, something he had done most of his life in
the ministry. He was looked upon as one of the very best
in our synod to stand up for the truth. Many times since
he died some of his colleagues have come up to me when
they are in the midst of doctrinal discussions and saying
they wish he were still around to help them.

Vacation to the Smokey Mountains
I think it was that first summer we were in Mankato that
Dad decided he and I should take a trip down to the
Smokey Mountains. Since Sarah and Marie were both
teaching in Iowa we made arrangements to have Joel stay
with them and attend school there while we were gone. It
was a beautiful trip and we really enjoyed having that time
together. It was the first we had been able to get away by

ourselves for that length of time. I don't remember how long we stayed, but it was beautiful scenery and was so nice to get away from all the daily work at home. Previous to that time the only trips the two of us had would be a day trip in the fall to Red Wing or perhaps to Henderson to take in the beautiful fall scenery. We would always pack a good picnic lunch for those one-day trips.

Rosemaling: There was a brief period when I got into the art of rosemaling. I always loved rosemaling and had my chance to learn a little bit about it when we lived on Marsh Street. My teacher, Dophrone Ogee, gave classes which I attended and really enjoyed. Sometimes classes were held at Lincoln School and occasionally at her home in North Mankato. With her help I managed to do a few pieces which are displayed here and there. The large plate I have hanging over my fireplace was one I hired her to do for Dad and me in honor of our 25th wedding anniversary which we had celebrated several years earlier.[3] Unfortunately he died before the rosemaled plate was completed. She noticed his name in the obituary column of the <u>Free Press</u> and felt so badly about it. I have treasured it these many years.

On my recent trip to California with Teddy I recognized quite a few of my pieces in the homes of Christine and Nancy. I remember sharing some pieces with them and it made me feel good to see they are enjoying them on their walls.

---

3   We received a beautiful curio as an anniversary gift from our family. Marie happened to be student teaching in Oshkosh, WI, at the time of our celebration and she got a ride home to Mankato with Prof. Isch.

In later years I discovered a lady in North Mankato named Grace Hewitt who was an excellent rosemaler and whenever I wanted a special gift I would go to her home and buy something. She told me one day that I was her best customer. My rosemaling means a lot to me whether I bought it or painted it myself. One of my last purchases from her was a rosemaled recipe box. That has a prominent spot in my kitchen.

Mom was Secretary I enjoyed my part-time secretary's job even though I only had a small typing desk in the corner of his office to begin with. However, there was part of a year that Dad was also president of Bethany College. In August of 1977 he was appointed acting President of Bethany Lutheran College, a job he held until March of 1978 when he found it necessary to resign from that position due to health reasons. During those few months Dad took over the office of the former president down at the end of the hall in the administrative wing. I then occupied the desk which was right outside his door there and carried on his seminary secretarial work.

The Move into the new Seminary Building.
As stated earlier, in June of 1978 the new seminary building was dedicated and the new seminary president's office was ready for occupancy. I got to take over the lovely secretary's office right outside the door of the president's office. The desk and furnishings were beautiful and I enjoyed my work there very much. However, with Dad's failing health, it was not altogether a happy time. Those years were tough – it is not easy to write about them.

Dad kept on with his teaching even when it was very difficult to make the trip to the seminary. The burden was heavy. As a family we did all that we could to keep him going. There were trips to Rochester - sometimes to be hospitalized. Thinking about those days we realize he had taken on too much – mainly the presidency of Bethany College. He was so capable but did not have the health to take on the extra duties of being college president.

On writing this I am so thankful for the outstanding job that Michael Muehlenhardt did when he wrote his M. Div. on Dad's life and work. It was not an easy task but when it was done we were all very well pleased. His siblings who were still living, John, Paul and Ingeborg all wrote letters to me telling how much they appreciated it. It is such a valuable source of information for our family, the greater Aaberg family, and many other friends and synod people as well.

Dad continued his duties as seminary president throughout 1978 and into early 1979. It got to be a very tough road to follow. Eventually we had to have medical oxygen delivered to our home and it became his "lifeline." He was trying to keep up his strength by riding his stationary bike for a few minutes every day. You children did your part helping with Dad's care at home. He got to thinking that a trip to Arizona might be just what he needed. Perhaps the drier climate would give his lungs a boost. It did not prove to be of benefit to him. I know I was not anxious to take that trip. I felt we needed the support of our family and friends here in Mankato, but I didn't want to stand in the way of making this last ditch effort at improving his health.

Every once in a while I have a chance to visit with some of the students who had Dad as their teacher for all three years of their seminary training. There was only one class that can say that and they are the ones we chose as pallbearers for the funeral.

Preparing for the Trip

Phil had made a box to house the portable oxygen unit on the floor of the back seat of our LTD. He was so proud of what his brother Phil had made for him and thought we should have it patented. We made arrangements for Marie, who was teaching at Saude at the time, to meet us at some crossroads down in Iowa where Dad's good friend Cubby Anderson met us bringing Marie with him so she could be our official chauffeur for the remainder of the trip. I did the driving from Mankato to that point. We made reservations at motels along the way ahead of time, of course. We also had to have medical oxygen delivered to us at those points to replenish the supply. If I remember right Dad was able to go into the restaurants with us for our meals. I need to mention that we made plans for Joel to stay with Pastor and Mrs. Wilhelm Petersen while we were gone. The All State Insurance logo comes to mind: *He was in good hands with the Petersens.* ☺

Arizona

There was a couple, John and Ethel Arends from our Luverne congregation, who wintered in Arizona and who also looked into suitable housing for us so there would be a place ready for us when we got there. It was a place called Savoy Plaza. It was pretty comfortable, had one bedroom, a living room, bathroom and kitchen. There was a nice swimming pool in the center of the Plaza which was surrounded by the rental units. Paul and Bea were lifesavers for us. They had gotten there before we arrived and had our unit supplied with food and whatever else might make it homier for us. I remember a beautiful green fern which they had hanging there on our patio. When we left to go home I gave it to some neighbors who had been especially nice to us since we could no way transport that home. At first Dad was able to ride in the car when we visited some places like the Arizona Lutheran School (WELS) and the general area around where we lived. I believe one day he was able to attend church services with us at the WELS mission we attended. The pastor there also came and gave us communion one day. Another day there were two ladies from the church who came to visit. We appreciated the visits very much.

Marie —Hat and Cowboy Boots

I know Phil had been in touch with Paul and ordered him to take Marie shopping for a cowboy hat. She really got a great hat. She bought some cowboy boots to complete the outfit which she still has. Marie was able to stay with us a week or so and was a big help with Dad and he loved having her there. We drove around getting groceries, etc. and, of course, seeing that medical oxygen was delivered every few days. I remember the fellow who delivered it showed us how to fill the small tank that Dad used when getting out and away from the house. I realize now how dangerous that was. We even kept using that connection when we got home again. It was pretty powerful moving oxygen from the big tank to the little one and we had to be sure we shut it off in time before it exploded. Thank goodness we got through that OK.

When it was time for Marie to get back to her teaching duties at Saude she dressed up in her new western gear for the plane ride. Good friends, Johnny and Dodie Anderson met her at the plane in Mason City, IA. This I remember: They took her to a bar and she had two Manhattans. She had endured quite a lot of turbulence over the Rocky Mountains so the drinks really helped settle her down. Thanks to those good friends.

Sarah comes down for Easter
It was so nice to look forward to Sarah's coming after Marie left. She was teaching at Parkland Lutheran School in Tacoma, WA, and took her Easter vacation to come to Arizona. I am pretty sure that John Arends took us to the airport in Phoenix to meet her. I was not familiar enough to drive to the airport but getting to the shopping centers was not a problem. Dad wanted me to go out and buy a new outfit while we were there. I did that and wore it quite a bit. It was a pale pink skirt with a cool light pink flowered top.

I brought my sewing machine along for something to do while I was sitting in the apartment complex. I was making a blue jacket which I still have hanging down in the basement. I don't know if I did a lot of sewing though. It just seemed like not the time to do it.

The decision to come home

Occasionally Dad would call some of his colleagues back in Mankato, B. W. Teigen, Reichwald, etc. One day I was sitting out by the pool for awhile and when I came in he told me he had called Paul Helland (faculty dean) at Bethany to get permission for Teddy to take a leave of absence from teaching for a few days. [4] Of course Paul readily agreed to that. So in a few days Teddy came out and again John Arends was put into service as our chauffeur from the airport.

Originally Dad had high hopes that he would get so much better out there and we would have Jon and Joel come after school was out and together we would drive to Parkland for a vacation. Eventually we would buy a home in Arizona – those were high hopes which never materialized. Our plans now changed and instead we would return to Mankato.

It probably didn't take too many days until Teddy came. I got everything packed up the best I could and we took off together with Phil's dandy oxygen carrier. One thing I remember most about the trip home was looking in the phone books as soon as we arrived at a motel to order the medical oxygen. Usually there was no problem with that. We made it a point to stop in fairly good-sized cities where we knew it would be available. That was an absolute necessity. I don't think that Dad was able to go into the restaurants much on the way home. We picked up food and brought it out to the car. It was not an easy trip and I am ever indebted to Teddy for being so kind and patient while we covered the miles each day bringing us closer to home.

4   Teddy taught American History and Sociology at Bethany College from '78 -'80 and again from '81-'83

At one point I remember Dad was especially nervous and asked Teddy to preach one of his sermons to him which he did.

The last night of the trip was especially hard as well as the day following which hopefully would be the last day of our journey. We stopped for lunch and Teddy went into the restaurant for lunch – later I joined him and he said he didn't think we would make it home that day. But we did. I can still remember driving up by the back door of our house on Marsh Street and what a good feeling that was. From Arizona Dad had called ahead to Marv Meyer and had him make sure there was a tank of oxygen at 909 Marsh. And there was! It was great to be home. I think Dad liked it, too, even though the health benefits he expected in Arizona had not materialized.

Joel was confirmed on May 27, 1979, by Pastor Wilhelm Petersen. Dad came with Marie to the church and sat in the back, but I don't think he was able to stay for the entire service. Orpha Storby and Mabel were at our house for dinner that day. Lester and Orpha Storby, Harry and Signe Olson, and Aunt Mabel Akre were Joel's sponsors at baptism.

Jonathan graduated from Martin Luther Academy in June of 1979. We were thrilled that he was picked to give the piano solo for the June night concert. He played *Toccata by Tauriello*. This was also mentioned in a section earlier when I was writing about music in our home but I refer to it here in connection with his graduation.

I don't know the exact time we came home from Arizona but it must have been springtime or early summer. Jonathan graduated from MLA, Sarah and Marie were both home for the summer. That was a tremendous help. Joel was home, and I suppose Jonathan was still working at Ben Franklin in New Ulm but was also at home some. At this time I don't know if Teddy was home or if he was sharing a house on Long Street with Dan Bruss as he did for some months.

Dad was in the hospital at Immanuel St. Joe's for a few days. We didn't take him down to Rochester anymore. The trip would have been too hard for him and there wasn't much that they could do. He had Dr. Seitzer for a doctor here and Dad was OK with that. I liked Dr. Seitzer since he was my doctor here and I always had received good care from him. He was a very compassionate doctor.

We were able to take care of Dad at home.
Sarah, being the good cook that she is, made good food for Dad without salt, as was a stipulation. I think at one point we even made lefse (without salt) for him thinking it would appeal to him. Marie was always a good help and Jonathan read for him some during the days. Joel did his part, too. He rigged up his telegraph set so Dad could buzz for him at night. It probably worked pretty well but sometimes it did not wake Joel up. Sarah, Marie and I took turns staying up with Dad at night. Not really staying up but sleeping on the davenport so we would hear him when we were needed. On our nights off two of us slept upstairs in the girls' bedroom. Dad could still give orders even though he was pretty sick. There were those elastic stockings that

he had to have on every morning and I remember him saying: "*I want my stockings on at 4:30 a.m. and breakfast after that – in that order.*" We were pretty tired at 4:30 in the morning but when Dad had been awake much of the night probably it didn't seem like an unreasonable request. We did the best we could. He continued to ride his stationery bike every day and was able with a little help to get up to use the bathroom.

Sarah was home from her teaching duties at Parkland for the summer and as her departure time to return to Washington was coming up she and Marie evidently talked it over and between the two of them decided that Sarah should stay home the fall semester of 1979. It was not met with the best of feelings out in Parkland, but they came around and she did get to stay home. I don't know what we would have done without her during this time. I was able to keep my job at the seminary which was so necessary. We received our health insurance through my employment there and as the years have played out it is easy to see how the Lord's hand has been with us all along in keeping things going for our family.

A few people from Bethany came over to visit, usually when they were invited. It wasn't always that Dad was up to company. I remember two of the last visitors he had were Justin and Orla Petersen and they were honored to be asked to come. Orla had been the longtime secretary to the president of the college and was extremely gifted in performing her role there.

Our Last Family Christmas Together

We had Christmas together at 909 Marsh Street and it was wonderful that we could. Dad got out into the living room and sat with us as we had our regular Christmas Eve family service. I got a lovely down-filled robe (Eddie Bauer) from Dad which kept me warm those long winter nights. I remember giving him a shirt for Christmas as I often did and also one of my special rosemaled boards.

Early in January he took a turn for the worse and it was on a Sunday afternoon that we got him into the hospital here in Mankato. We all visited him there and it was Jonathan and I who went to see him that last evening which would have been a Monday evening. He kissed me as we left and said, *"I love you."* I told him I loved him too. His words to Jonathan were *"Go with God and be a good boy."* Marie and I went to the hospital in the morning and met with the doctor; the prognosis was not good. Since Dad was sleeping we decided to go home for a few minutes and would return soon. Shortly after we arrived home we got a call that he had been taken to his eternal rest. Marie and I went back to the hospital. Teddy arrived at the hospital having come from Albert Lea. Just the evening before Joel took the bus back to Prairie du Chien and that morning Sarah had taken Jonathan over to New Ulm. Somehow we got word to her and she brought Jonathan home again. I called Pres. Oscar Siegler, a good friend of Dad's at Prairie du Chien, and asked him to share this hard, sad news with Joel. It was hard news for him to hear way down there by himself.[5] Arrangements were made so someone from there

---

5   Joel had started as a freshmen in high school at Prairie du Chien the fall of 1979.

brought Joel to Rochester where Marv Meyer met him and brought him home.

The end came on January 8, 1980. It was a long, hard struggle for Dad but he had the amazing ability to keep going all those years in spite of such a debilitating illness. He could not have done it and accomplished so much without the support of his entire family – all of you children in your own role. It was not a single one but all of us together that were able to keep our family going through all these years with the Lord's help, of course. I often think how Dad could keep his spirits up which helped all of us to carry on. He accomplished much for his synod and left quite a legacy for his family. We must all remember that.

The Aaberg Family in 1976
Sarah, Marie, Jon, Ted, Joel
Melvina, Theodore

The funeral was at Mt. Olive with Pastor Wilhelm Petersen preaching. Teddy also gave a short greeting to the congregation. That was nice. The members of Dad's seminary class, which he had for nearly three years, were the pallbearers with the exception of Craig Ferkenstad who was stranded in Wisconsin because of a snowstorm. John Wilde took his place and that was fine since he was also a special friend of our family. I know that Matthew Luttman was vicaring at a congregation in Missouri and we paid for his airline ticket to come home. He told us he would not have missed it.

Paul, Phil, and John were there from the Aaberg family. Earlier Ida, Ingeborg, and Herman came to visit. I remember that Marvin's wife Terry came for the funeral; also my brothers Leonard and Orlando braved the bitter storm and drove down from Tracy. I think maybe Myrtle and her husband Roy were there or else it was Viola and Bob. My oldest brother Gerhard (Gay) died some weeks before Ted did. Now all my brothers are gone, but he was the first.

&

Chapter Three

~ Recent Years ~

❧

A new chapter in my life without my dear husband whom I loved very much. To this day when some memories of Ted come up I get a warm feeling. I never wanted anyone to take his place.

Life had to go on. First and foremost, when all the funeral matters were taken care of we needed to find a place we could call home.

As I was working with Wilbur Lieske on our taxes for 1980 he said, "*Well, Ted made it into the New Year*" which was of benefit for us in that respect. Dad always had done the taxes but that was out of his hands now and I took over. I always liked working with figures and it was a good thing because that was not as difficult for me as it might have been.

Buying a House

We always lived in parsonages or a synod-owned home as we did in Mankato. The Trustees and Regents were very patient with me. They were not pushing us to hurry and get out of the house at 909 Marsh Street, although they were probably wondering how I was going to do it. Marie and I got in touch with Century 21 and made several visits to homes on the market in the hilltop area. We weren't pleased with any of them. Some looked in pretty bad shape and in one house on Homer Street animals came running out from under the chairs, sofas, etc. Some were also out of our price range.

We got a break when I visited with Mrs. Harriet Schwarz after Bible Class in Mt. Olive one Sunday morning. She told me they were going to be selling their home and moving to an assisted living place up in the Minneapolis area, but this wouldn't be until August. A few years earlier Dad and I and Joel had been invited over to the Schwarz's for supper one evening so I was familiar with the home and I loved it. No way did I think we would be able to afford it. It was much nicer than anything I had envisioned. I called Phil Aaberg and talked to him about it. He told me to find out what their price was. And so I did. They had it listed for $64,000.

Shortly after the funeral Paul Tweit came over to the house with a check for $15,000 from the Synod's insurance plan for pastors. In addition to that we had some money in the bank since I was receiving payments from the 1/2 farm I had inherited from Uncle Olaf. It happened at that time that you could get 17% interest on money invested for 6 months. If only we could get that today! Phil called Lester Schwarz and had a very nice visit with him – I think they talked about everything from finances to church matters and they really saw eye to eye on many things. So Phil gave me the thumbs up to go ahead and make the deal. I believe I paid $5000 security money to hold the house for us. And in August we paid another $35,000 making a $40,000 down payment.

I remember calling Rev. Milton Tweit who was chairman of the Board of Regents at that time and asked if my family and I could reside in the house on Marsh Street until August and he was very agreeable to that. I am sure it was a load off their shoulders, too, and certainly mine. All I can say is the Lord was looking out for us big time. I am sure Dad had worried about where we would live, how we would make a go of it, etc. He was way too sick to even talk about it those last weeks. Earlier we had driven around Mankato and gotten a glimpse of some homes from the car but that was it.

Phil made a quick trip to Mankato to give the house a good once over and then together with Mr. and Mrs. Schwartz we went down to the Schwarz's lawyer's office. We set up a 15-year Contract for Deed at 8% interest and I paid $229.36 a month for 15 years. At the conclusion of this time the house was ours. We invited the neighbors and a few close friends to join in our celebration with a Mortgage Burning Party on August 16, 1995. That time had gone pretty fast now that I think about it.

Mr. Wilbur Lieske was a big help to me with my finances also. He got some good deals for me where I could invest some available funds at no risk and at a really good rate of interest. That helped me a lot. He also was my tax consultant for quite a few years until he found it necessary to get out of the business because of ill health.

It was very exciting purchasing a home. It is a beautiful home in a nice neighborhood. Having such great neighbors who became wonderful friends has been an added blessing all these years. I continued to work at the seminary and as I was looking back at some of my accounts I saw I didn't really make that much money – about $350 a month at first. But it was the Social Security which kicked in that saved us. I still can never understand why some of the seminary students decided to opt out of Social Security thinking they can invest that money and do better on their own. I hope it's working out for them especially now during this time when our country is in a financial crisis.

I think I fell into the role of being a homeowner quite easily. It was a good feeling. I think some of my friends over at Bethany were kind of surprised that it happened so fast. They were happy for our family and congratulated me on being a homeowner. As I referred to earlier there always seemed to be enough money for my expenses. Sometimes I would compare myself to the woman in the Bible whose cruz of oil never ran empty. I give God the credit for that. I always loved accounting in school and learned to keep good records – especially when Joel and Jon were still in school and I had to make sure they were being taken care of and I wasn't pocketing their share for my own personal benefit. But thinking it over I kind of wonder if Jonathan was maybe in charge of his own Social Security check from the very beginning. Poor Joel was still under his mother's thumb, but not for long.

Jonathan was a student at Dr. Martin Luther College and continuing to work at the Ben Franklin Store. Joel had finished his first year at Prairie du Chien and starting his second.

Dad told me one of those last days that if he couldn't see Joel through Prairie du Chien he hoped someone else would. Those were hard years for Joel being that far from home and I am very sorry for that, but there are good things that he learned those years which can never be taken away from him. He made some very good friendships, friends whom I still come in contact with occasionally and who always inquire about Joel and ask me to relay their greetings to him.

As the years went on he got to be quite a basketball player and things got better. He acquired the nickname (Joey) then, especially used when they were cheering from the stands for him to do his slam-dunks – even backward dunks sometimes. He was also good at blocking shots. Marie and I got to see some games at Prairie du Chien and also went to the tournaments in Wisconsin. I believe she was teaching in Scarville at this time. We saw a lot of games and they were some of the fondest memories and most exciting times that I can remember. Sarah was also there for one of those tournaments. I think it was before she and Ron were married. She was teaching at Parkland Lutheran School in Washington at the time. John and Brenda came down from Chicago for one of the games. It was nice to have them there.

Marie receives a Certificate of Outstanding Service from the Governor of Iowa, August 23, 1978.
I have been weaving in and out in this Journal taking note of special events in the lives of my children and, of course, Marie is mentioned throughout but I want to concentrate on a special event in her life here. As mentioned earlier her first year of teaching was at Saude Lutheran School in Iowa. The school was a little building similar to what you might read about in the magazine published today called _Reminisce_. There was a big stove where the pupils could warm their lunches or dry their wet mittens after playing in the snow. It was similar to the first school I taught at in Norseland in 1947. There was no indoor plumbing and she tells about the girls' outhouse door that was kept closed by pulling a milk can up against it as you entered. It was a rather hard year in a number of ways.

Now for a very special event which happened the last day at the school picnic. It was customary to have a bike hike followed by a picnic at the Saude Park. The pupils could go wading and have water fights in the creek which was usually shallow. While Marie was a short distance away in the parking lot, one of the pupils came up the bank yelling, _"Miss Aaberg, Jeff's drowning!"_ Sure enough, he was! Jeff Knutson was floating face down having stepped into an unexpected deep pothole probably formed from an earlier spring heavy rain. The pupils standing on the shore, with the exception of the two Webster boys, were frozen stiff as far as being able to help, and the park attendant rather than help said he would go call the sheriff and tell him there had been a drowning. Jeff was a huge boy – Marie and the Webster boys were able to drag him to a sandbar where Marie quickly began to apply the life-saving technique called mouth-to-mouth resuscitation. God be praised! His eyes started to bug out, he began to cough up water from his lungs and threw up. Marie saved his life! How fortunate that she had been taught this life-saving technique at college. Jeff graduated from Christian Day School that same evening and was confirmed that next Sunday. His family surprised Marie with a beautiful plaque thanking her for saving Jeffrey's life. Not only that – she received an award from the Governor of Iowa at the state fair that summer. Marie, Dad and I along with Jonathan and Joel made the trip to Des Moines. Dad was determined to go even though he was in very poor health at the time.

After two years in Saude she received and accepted a call from Scarville Lutheran School which she herself had attended. Those years were especially made pleasant because of Signe Olson who kept an eye out for Marie. When bad weather was forecast she would call Marie and invite her to come down since Marie's home was a trailer on the church property. There was always plenty of fun times and great food at Signe's. I should also mention they played a lot of Yahtze. When Marie's trailer caught fire one spring she was pleased to get to stay with Signe for six weeks while the trailer was repaired.

Marie Accepts Call to Mt. Olive

Her next call was to Mt. Olive in Mankato to teach 5th and 6th grades. I can still remember when Marie and I were standing in the kitchen that Sunday morning waiting for a phone call from the School Board informing us who was to be called. Soon Oren Quist called and Marie was the one and we were both rejoicing! That was the beginning of 20 very productive years of teaching for the Mt. Olive congregation. She continues to be fondly remembered by the parents and many of the pupils for the fine quality of teaching which was always evident in her classroom. Four of her former Mt. Olive pupils, all National Merit Scholarship winners, submitted her name to Who's Who in America's Teachers while they were high school seniors. She has four brass-plated plaques attesting to this hanging on the wall in her home office. She knows the names of three of the students: Luke Asleson, Kendra Kessel, and Julie Westphal – one student was anonymous.

I found this article which I had printed in one of my former Christmas letters and thought it appropriate to quote here:

> Marie got a real thrill in her teaching career this fall when her class won a state-wide competition in Minnesota sponsored by Best Buy, Target, the Tribune and the Minnesota Vikings. The project consisted of lesson plans each week called "Gridiron Geography" and the production of a 12-foot long U. S. map showing what they had learned. They won a trip to Winter Park, the Vikings training facility, and were treated "royally." There were 680 teachers and 18,000 pupils who participated so it was really very special.

I was busy working at the seminary and synod offices and she at Mt. Olive. Marie and I took some great trips during those years which I will write about in another section.

Mom's Work Continues:
The last several years had been difficult for our family, but I was blessed with a wonderful family and many great friends and relatives. Times weren't so hard. I had a job which was so important in more ways than one. I can't explain all the blessings that have come my way because of my work at the Seminary and later for the Evangelical Lutheran Synod.

I always liked typing, accounting and shorthand in addition to algebra and geometry which were some of my favorites in high school. When I was young I used to think I would like to be a beauty operator or a secretary. Never did I think of being a teacher, but it turned out that decision led me down the best road of all. If I hadn't been a teacher I would never have met Dad and I wouldn't have had you children. My family are my *"crown jewels,"* the joys of my life.

Being wife of Pres. Theodore A. Aaberg, and author of *A City Set on a Hill* always held me in good stead with visitors and dignitaries from other synods in the US and abroad. It was sort of a feather in my cap and I was, and am, still proud of it.

Mom as Full-time Secretary
That first year after Dad passed away I roomed and boarded a seminary student, Dan Larson. It was nice to have a little extra income and have someone around the house. I

went to work about nine in the morning, usually brought my lunch which I ate in the student lounge with the seminary students. After Joel graduated from Prairie du Chien and was attending Bethany he also came over for lunch. It was a pleasant lunch hour and we had lots of fun. Joel lived at home those two Bethany years. I thought he had had enough of dorm life after 4 years in Prairie du Chien. We were just talking one evening how he enjoyed coming over and eating with the students. He especially enjoyed it when Juul Madson ate there with us. Those are special days to remember.

The Seminary Under new Leadership

When Dad was sick and could not continue his work at the seminary, Glenn Reichwald was the acting president until the Board of Regents called Wilhelm Petersen to be the new president. The evening of the same day Bill received his Call he phoned me at our Marsh Street home where we still lived and asked me to stay on as his secretary. I was so happy that he requested me and I accepted immediately, That was a win/win situation for both of us. I needed the security of a job and he needed help to become acquainted with the operation of the seminary president's office. Working with Dad I had learned how to do many things that would assist the new president in his role. They weren't just mundane chores like typing letters, greeting visitors, answering the phone, making coffee, etc., but many other very important tasks. At the time I didn't realize how much I had learned from Dad and how it would benefit me throughout my 28 years of full-time service to the seminary and later the Evangelical Lutheran Synod. I think one of the things Bill appreciated most was my help putting together the report for the Board of Regents which met four times a year.

The Regents were the governing body and there was always some apprehension that went along with those meetings. Using the same format as Dad had used, I was able to put into rough draft a lot of the information that was expected for those meetings. What I couldn't do I just left blank for the president to fill in. Bill would type his additions to the report and return it to me for putting the final copy together in preparation for the meeting. Bill usually came back pretty relieved when the meeting was over. He would often tell me that the Regents were very pleased with the report. It was a joint effort and it made me feel good to be able to be a part of this important work. I had been well trained by my husband.

Filling out applications requesting money from the Aid Association for Lutherans and Lutheran Brotherhood organizations was another duty that required a lot of work. Good record keeping was a must and I was good at that. We could request money from those organizations for scholarships or funding for seminary workshops, etc. It was one thing to request the money but after we had used the money it was necessary to put out a very detailed account of how the money was spent. That's where the good record keeping comes in. If we wanted to keep getting money we had to make sure we were using it wisely.

I need to make mention here of the AAL's yearly dinner party they put on for the seminary seniors each year. For many years it was held at the Country Pub, a well-known

country restaurant outside of St. Peter. We loved those parties. The seniors were in charge of providing a little entertainment for the guests – usually they were quite good. But
one year I especially remember was when Jim Krikava, who
was a musician in addition to his other many talents, sang a
song entitled "*The Seminary is Run by Melvina*" sung to the
tune of Elvira.[1] The AAL always presented the seniors with
a gift of an individual communion set for making home
visits. In addition they also gave me some wonderful gifts
as tokens of appreciation for whatever I had to do with the
arrangements. I have several pewter mementos: a candy
dish, candle holder, picture frame, a beautiful desk clock
and letter opener to name a few. I love and cherish them all
and have them displayed in my home.

I always enjoyed serving tea to the president every afternoon at 3 PM. At first it was a cookie or a kringla, which
was a favorite. Later when the president was trying to
watch his sweets it went down to half a cookie. It always
made the afternoons go smoothly. He was good at re-
minding me to go to church on Sunday ☺. I could figure
that as a given – and then of course for Lenten services and
Advent services it was the same. I never received a harsh
word from him nor was I ever turned down when I wanted
to take some time off or leave early. I had the perfect job,
and I value those days as some of the most pleasant of my
working career. He and his wife Naomi always included

---

1 " Peggy and I wrote a song for Melvina that we sang for
an AAL dinner for the seminary class in 1983. It was set to the hit
country song by the Oak Ridge Boys entitled, *Elvira*. Our song was
called, "Melvina." Afterward she told Peggy that her name was finally
just the right one for some good fun."

me in festivities at their home which had to do with seminary or synod work.

Juul Madson

I had other duties in addition to being Pres. Petersen's secretary. Juul Madson, who was Greek professor at the seminary this entire time, was also College Chaplain for many
years. During this time I was in charge of putting out the
worship folder each week. By Friday afternoon, hopefully
earlier rather than later, he would have the hymn numbers
and other information to me so I could go ahead with the
folder. The organists over at the college were waiting for
the hymn numbers so they could practice over the weekend. That was usually the last order of the day on Fridays.
For many of these folders Jonathan provided attractive and
fitting cover designs according to the church year. That
really put the final touches on. I appreciated that so much
and Juul really liked them too – one of Jonathan's many
talents. I have kept all these designs and reminisce about
those days when I come across them. I have copies of all of
them in my files at home.

Juul Madson was also secretary of the synod's Doctrine
Committee for all the years that I can remember. He
would rough out the minutes on his typewriter and give
them to me for typing up the final copy. This was another job I could do. Juul was known for being an excellent
grammarian and I learned a lot from him. Proper punctuation was another of his specialties. In addition I found
out everything they talked about at their meetings and as a
secretary I was aware of the importance of confidentiality.
I was always interested in our synod's doctrinal discussions.

It was an education for me. I always relied on Juul when I had questions about grammar or punctuation. Of course on the things he had written, it was always correct. Now years later when I am working in the Archives and I come across Juul's files I find all kinds of markings with a red pen on papers and letters he has gotten from other people. He could not resist making corrections on their work. I don't think he got too bored at committee meetings because he could take care of some editing. It gives me a chuckle now when I see all these red markings he made. I need to add a P.S. to the typing of the Doctrine Committee Minutes. The computers had come in and I eventually had a chance to get Juul started on an Apple computer. It wasn't long before he did his own minutes. He told me one day, *"Now you won't find out what we talked about anymore."* Juul took to the computer like a duck to water. I may have used this expression about myself somewhere in this journal. He loved that computer and tried everything. Some of the others I have tried to teach have not gotten that far. His family gives me credit for getting him started. For one of his birthdays they gave him a computer. I received many gifts as tokens of appreciation at Christmas time from Juul and Clarice. He was a very kind, thoughtful and caring gentleman and I am one of many who really miss him. He was taken to his eternal rest shortly after Easter in 2008. Not too many weeks before he was over using my Apple computer to put out his year-end letter. I served him coffee and treats when he was here, of course.

Special Perks There were some very special perks that came with being the seminary secretary – the students. The interaction with these students has been a major source of joy for me. I have become very fond of many, I could even say most of them. They have been a real source of comfort and joy throughout all the 28 years that I have worked in close communication with them. In the seminary building on Division Street they walked past my window every time they went to class. On Secretary's Day I often got a special gift from them, flowers, vases, jewelry to name a few – all treasured gifts. Some of them would often sit down in the big soft chairs in my office to chat. To this day I still receive Christmas cards from several of them. And I must add that I still get hugs from many of them when they return to Mankato for the annual Synod Conventions in June.

I need to write about a few of the seminary students who did over and above what you would expect them to do. They were Jon Bruss and James Krueger - both of them were very good construction workers, especially Jim since he did that for a living before entering seminary and also worked at it while he attended seminary. Jon was a really smart and good guy who also had building experience and could do anything. It happened that after I consulted with Uncle Paul, also sending pictures to him, etc., it was decided that it might not be a bad idea to have my roof reshingled. These two guys volunteered to do the job. I fixed some quick lunches for them while they were working up there and I don't remember exactly how much I paid them, but for me it was very reasonable I am sure. The roof is holding up very well. Who could expect a couple of seminary students to do that for the secretary? Only once since did Jon Bruss have to crawl up the little opening in my closet to get up in the attic and check on something. [2]

2   It turns out that in the year 2010 my roof suffered some hail damage and thankfully the insurance company agreed to pay a

Jim Krueger also built a beautiful Scandinavian cupboard for my kitchen. Rachel Anthony drew the plans for it and he built it. It is one of my most treasured pieces of furniture. He is a pastor in the Wisconsin Synod at a church in Stoddard, Wisconsin. His pastoral work is a great blessing to any congregation he serves.[3]

I also want to mention Terry Schultz and his wife Mary – missionaries to Peru for several years now. He is a great missionary and has always been a great friend and confidant for me. I can't say enough about a person like Terry. He is one in a million – many souls have been saved, and continue to be saved because of the work of Terry Schultz and his wife Mary. Much of it pretty scary work in the jungles. They lay their lives on the line many times I am sure – especially Terry. He puts out a publication regularly – once a month or so – called "Jungle Journal." He writes about his work in the jungle in such vivid style you can't help but be swept into the great mystery of the jungle and urgency of the mission work that is carried on there. [4]

Tor Jakob Welde, a seminary student from Norway, came to the seminary in 1999 with his lovely wife Reiko and daughter Miriam. They are precious friends and will be mentioned in more detail later.

substantial amount to have it reshingled which will happen sometime in the spring of 2011.

3   Since I keep in touch with Jim and his family at Christmas I learned he is now serving a WELS congregation in Medford, WI.

4   Sadly I learned that Terry and Mary no longer work full-time for the ELS mission in Peru, but will return on a part-time basis. They are now working for the Wisconsin Synod in the Dominican Republic and also Haiti.

Mom becomes secretary to the Synod President, George Orvick

Up to this time my energies were devoted mostly to being secretary to the president of the seminary. But in 1987 it became evident that the ELS synod office required the work of a full-time president. Rev. George Orvick had been pastor of The Church of the Holy Cross in Madison, Wisconsin, for many years and also served as president of the ELS simultaneously. In 1987 the office of synod president was moved to the seminary building on Division Street in Mankato. A certain amount of remodeling was done to make an adequate office and boardroom to carry on the synodical business. My office stayed the same, of course, but now a considerable amount of duties were added to my workload. When anticipating this change I was a little nervous, wondering how I would do with all of these important duties – after all – here I was, secretary to the *seminary president as well as the synod president.* I must say that "I took to it like a duck to water." I loved it. I was able to handle the transition quite well. It was good for me to have more work to do and I think whatever Pres. Orvick asked of me I was able to carry out. In the boardroom of our new Seminary/Synod building where the meetings were held there was a little button under the table where Pres. Orvick sat. If he needed anything from his office files he just pressed that button and I would hear it buzz at my desk. I would promptly go into the boardroom to get his message and I think nearly always I was able to come up with whatever he was requesting. Of course, there again, I owe a lot to Dad for what I had learned from him.

This work entailed putting out a lot more letters and reports. I always enjoyed typing and I was provided with an excellent typewriter and copy machine and in due time the **Computer**. I also did quite a bit of research, which I loved to do, in preparation of reports for the synod meetings. Extensive reports were put out documenting many events that took place like installations and anniversaries of pastors, anniversaries of congregations, Christian Day School teachers' years of service, etc. Deaths of pastors and pastors' widows who had died during the year were recorded and a service recognizing them was always held in June at the convention. I'd say anything worth reporting was reported. When you start talking about the affairs of the synod there is just too much to mention and what I say is only a "drop in the bucket."

There were several controversies during the time I served and much bitterness developed in certain parts of the synod because of that. The main ones were **The Church and the Ministry, Church Fellowship, The Sacrament of the Altar, The Role of Women in the Church, and Apologetics.** Fortunately growing up in a good Christian home, a conservative congregation and having had good pastors for my confirmation instruction I had been well educated on these topics before I became so involved in the work of the church. Thankfully I was on the same page as my supervisors and also the same page as Dad would have been I am sure. When you are dedicated to keeping the Word of the Lord in it's truth and purity those unpleasant things are unavoidable. As secretary I got in on a lot of it. But one thing I am grateful for is that Dad was spared from as much as he was. He had worked very hard during his good years and not so good years trying to bring some harmony into those bitter debates. He had endured a lot of controversy during his years of service and every once in awhile I still hear how pastors wish he were still around to help them with tough meetings. It was easier for me that he didn't have to suffer through that any longer. He had done enough. In my role as secretary I could just go home at night and get away from it.

Pres. Orvick was an excellent synod president, preacher and leader as well as a wonderful person to work for. I learned a lot from him about the affairs of the synod while I was his secretary. He was always kind to me and thoughtful. I drove my little blue Mustang around town, sometimes to the FedEx office in North Mankato or up the hill to Kinko's Printing - now days they will come to our office and pick up special mailings or projects. I will probably always be known for the baked goods I prepared for the meetings or just as a special treat for afternoon coffee. All these things, of course, I was happy to do and to a lesser degree am still doing.

Office equipment: The computers came in and brought a new era of technology and communication to my office. I don't remember which year exactly. I think Wilbur Lieske brought in the first one. Although I enjoyed getting it I don't believe I used it too long before John Sehloff got me set up with an Apple computer, a brand which I totally am sold on to this day. The IT Department at Bethany College has always been good at updating my computer or replacing with a new one as time goes on. They also are only a phone call away when I need help. If it can't be done over the phone they make a personal visit to the office. I tell my friends re: the computer I have at home – *It is like having another person in the house.* I often think of how I typed Dad's book, _A City Set On A Hill_, twice on an old Underwood typewriter – however, he rented an electric typewriter for me to use for the later part of it. What a blessing it would have been to have a computer then. I think Dad would have taken to the computer had he lived to use one.

Other equipment we have gotten so used to nowadays are the fax machine, copy machine, electric staplers, black and white and color printers, postage machines, letter folders, paper cutters, paper shredders, etc., etc. Whole books are even being scanned into copy machines and computers. Lots of paper is being used and lots of it is being wasted as well. Thankfully some of it gets recycled. When a person has grown up during the Depression you really notice how wasteful our country has become.

Social life for the secretaries. While visiting recently with my good friend Audrey Winkler, who has been a very efficient receptionist for Bethany College for many years, we talked about a "club" the secretaries used to have called the "Sew and Sew's" which met maybe once a month or so. Now it seems everyone is too busy. But we took turns in each other's homes where we got together and maybe sewed a little, visited a lot, and always had a very tasty snack to top it all off and also some wine. We didn't do much sewing, but a few people brought some things to work on as I remember. Delores Fisher was the "super secretary" at the college who kept us all in line. She couldn't resist looking over everything we handed out and checking it for "mis-takes." She often found many. It was her thing ☺. She always wore high-heeled shoes and dressed as for any fashion magazine. She and I always shared a room when Bethany hosted "retreats" years ago. She was a true friend to me. Sadly I heard her funeral was attended by only about 20 people with no one officially representing Bethany College for her many years of excellent service there. However, Audrey, who had visited Delores occasionally during her later years, attended and offered some remarks in honor of Delores. The funeral was not held in Mankato where she had lived, worked, and was a church member for many years. I am sure that contributed to the lack of attendance by staff at Bethany College and other friends.

Back to the family
Teddy attended Princeton Theological Seminary in New Jersey for one year and graduated from there on **June 2, 1981, with a Masters of Theology Degree**. Marie and I attended the ceremony traveling by both plane and train as I remember. I don't know how we made all those connections but Teddy mapped it all out for us and we made it. He made arrangements for us to stay in the dorm at no cost to us and we appreciated that. We were, of course, very proud to be there for this important accomplishment in his education. He took us into New York City one day on the train. That is the only time I have been to New York City. I remember seeing a large group of Jewish men in black suits and hats walking along the sidewalk. We also got to the top of the IDS building and looked around the city and over towards the Statue of Liberty so proudly standing in the harbor there. I will note here that we also saw an

exact replica (except much smaller) of that famous statute in Norway when we were there the summer of 2006. [5]

Sarah had been teaching in Parkland since 1978. Accepting the call to Parkland Lutheran School brought her into "Aaberg country." This made it pretty exciting for our family. Grandma Alette had passed away before this time. However, Herman and Paul and Bea as well as Randolf, Ingeborg and her family, plus other cousins, etc. were there so she had plenty of relatives around.

They had joint ELS/WELS teacher/pastoral conferences at certain times during the year in Washington. This is how she met her future husband Ron. I remember a letter came to my home in Mankato with an unfamiliar return address on the envelope. It turned out it was a letter Ron was trying to get to Sarah and which I, of course, forwarded to her. She was so pleased to get the letter and a budding romance was in the works. I noticed on her next trip home she was wearing a beautiful opal necklace. Paul and Bea were at my home visiting at that time and were with me when we picked her up at the airport. Paul figured out that *she was in love.* And she was. We began to hear more and more about Ron and how his parents had come out to Washington to meet her. I know she prepared a meal for them while they were there. She was probably pretty nervous about that but you know Sarah's cooking skills, I am sure it was wonderful, and they have only gotten better.

As time went on they became engaged and a future wedding was in the works. Of course our family was happy that

5   Norway has the best copper in the world and that's where the copper came from for our Statue of Liberty.

Sarah had found a fine Christian helpmeet in Ron. We looked forward to meeting him and after some time – not too long a time – when he asked for her hand in marriage I readily gave my approval. It was fun for us to get into the business of planning a wedding.

Showers: I had forgotten how many Ladies Aids had honored her with showers: Linda Teigen hosted a personal shower at her home, and bridal showers were put on by Mt. Olive, Scarville, Norwegian Grove, and Norseland. Nowadays that is almost a thing of the past. It is usually up to some family members or friends to organize a shower.

Sarah made her own wedding gown and it was beautiful with Norwegian hardanger on the bodice and headpiece. She worked very hard on that and I know some of the ladies with whom she became good friends at Parkland were very interested in her wedding gown and probably helped her with some of it. When the school year was over Sarah had to think about getting all the things she had accumulated back to Minnesota. Fortunately Linda Teigen, who had become a good friend to our family and to Sarah, arranged for her father who was out in the Washington area skiing to come by and pick up her stuff and transport it back to our home. I don't know how we would have gotten that done if it hadn't been for his generosity and Linda's arranging it.

They were married on Easter Sunday, April 18, 1982. It was a family affair with Marie as maid of honor and Ron's sister Shirleen and sister-in-law as bridesmaids. Ron's brother Randy was best man, Jonathan and Joel were groomsmen, and brother Ted was the preacher. Don Hahnke, Ron's brother-in-law, sang the Lords Prayer, and Corey Hahnke was the ring bearer. There was someone who was not from the family, however, and that was Katie Wood who was the flower girl. Margaret Annexstad, a fantastic organist and friend, provided the music.

A reception was held in the church basement. It is only fitting that I mention Rachel Anthony here since she was the all-around person in charge of making sure everything was beautiful. Paul and Phil had so many daffodils and tulips sent from the West Coast for the occasion that Rachel commented to me . . . *for once I had more flowers than I knew what to do with.* In order to add some entertainment for the guests who were enjoying the refreshments, Jonathan sat at the piano and played several pieces. Uncle Marvin, Christine and Bill, Nancy and Phil, and children were along from California. I do want to tell about Marvin and Phil polishing up the Model A and getting it in good working condition so it could be used to transport the bride and groom back to Mankato after the festivities were over. That all worked out very well and it was so neat that the '29 Model A could be used. Dad would have liked that.

When all the festivities were over at the church, the family and close relatives on both sides came to our home and the bride and groom got busy opening their gifts. That's always a fun part. I know that Nancy and Christine were busy in the kitchen and served some tasty snacks for us to enjoy. When the evening was over Sarah and Ron took off on their honeymoon to places unknown. We had all enjoyed a wonderful day and were well pleased with the celebration of their wedding.

After the wedding they were at home in West Bend, Wisconsin where Ron taught Latin and religion and also was a track coach at Kettle Moraine Lutheran High School. Sarah made use of her sewing abilities and got a job at a local fabric/sewing store in West Bend.

By **June 1983 Joel was a senior at Prairie du Chien and ready for graduation**. What a great and happy day that was! Most of the family was able to be there, but I am not sure about Teddy . . . he will remember. Sarah was expecting a baby at the time and Ron brought her as far as Prairie du Chien. After the celebration she returned with us to Mankato. I prepared a picnic lunch which we enjoyed on the campus grounds. It was a beautiful campus and a wonderful graduation celebration.

Rare Book Collection Memorial for Dad. Teddy was teaching at Bethany for some years after he was through at Our Savior's in Albert Lea. He was also taking classes prior to obtaining his Master's Degree in Library Science from MSU, as it was known at that time—now called Minnesota State University, Mankato. The title of the project was called: *A Descriptive Study and Rare Book Collection with Accompanying Guidelines for the Bethany Seminary Rare Book Collection.* This was dated December 1983. He was instrumental in getting the seminary's valuable Rare Book Collection cataloged and contained in the computer database of OCLC, a non-profit cataloging service, headquartered in Columbus, Ohio. He also designed a brochure as a memorial to Dad entitled *Rare Book Collection* which includes a nice picture of Dad. I would like to mention Mary Birmingham who was Bethany College librarian and for whom Teddy worked several years while a student. She was a big help to him I know and also became a good friend to our family. Marie remembers that Dad complimented Mary Birmingham saying she could become the governor of the state. Working for her probably helped to encourage and foster Teddy's talent for research which served him so well in his future employment in various key positions at Harvard University and others entities.

On December 9, 1983, Teddy graduated from Mankato State University with a Master of Science Degree in Library Media Education. I was proud to be in attendance at the graduation exercises. If I remember correctly I had Dr. and Mrs. Balcziak, Mary Birmingham, and probably Pres. and Mrs. B. W. Teigen as dinner guests that evening. Louella Balcziak was his advisor, I believe. These days I shy away from entertaining such dignitaries, but I guess I had a little more confidence in my cooking skills than I do today.[6] He worked as reference librarian at Concordia Theological Seminary in Fort Wayne, Indiana, from 1984-1986. Dr. Robert Preus hired him and he reported to Cameron MacKenzie, the director of the library. His primary duty was to help theological students with their master's theses. One semester he taught a class in Reformation History which he enjoyed.

---

6   Teddy's graduation from MSU got a little out of order here but I thought it worked out best since I wanted to write about my first three granddaughters next.

Beginning information of my first three granddaughters.

On August 7, 1983, Jennifer Ann made her appearance - quite by surprise since she was not expected so soon nor was she expected to be conceived along with her twin brother Ronald, who was taken to be with the Lord even before he was born. The Lord moves in mysterious ways.

It was on a Sunday morning when we got the news. Although it was very sad to hear the news about baby Ronald, we rejoiced at the birth of baby Jennifer. I can't say how delighted I was to be a grandmother. We went to church that morning with the news. It took awhile for it all to sink in - the loss of a grandson yet the joy of having a healthy granddaughter. The Lord moves in ways beyond our understanding.

Special highlights about the Mehlberg granddaughters.

Jennifer Ann was confirmed on May 17, 1998, graduated from Kettle Moraine Lutheran High School as Salutatorian on June 2, 2002, and from Martin Luther College in May of 2007, with a double major: Elementary Education and a 5-year degree in Early Childhood. She received a Call to Crown of Life Lutheran School, Fort Myers Florida to be director and teach early childhood. Something special from Jennie's early years: I received the following from the USAA (United States Achievement Academy):

"Your grandchild JENNIFER MEHLBERG has been named a UNITED STATES ACHIEVEMENT ACADEMY NATIONAL AWARD WINNER. This is a position of honor less than 10% of all young people can ever hope to attain, placing your grandchild among our nation's most elite youth."

SHAWNA MARIE made her grand entrance on May 9, 1985. She and Jennie being so close in age have always shared a lot of wonderful experiences growing up - sports for one thing - especially volleyball —taking the championships for their Kettle Moraine volleyball team many times. Shawna was confirmed on May 16, 1999, graduated from Kettle Moraine Lutheran High School as Valedictorian on June 1, 2003, and from Martin Luther College in May of 2008 with a double major: Elementary Education and a 5-year degree in Early Childhood. She then received a Call to teach at Divine Savior Academy in Doral, Florida.

Something special about Shawna from early years as reported in the West Bend Paper: Eleven-*year old Shawna Mehberg's first flight was short, but maybe that's best, since she described it as bumpy and a little scary. She was one of more than 70 youths, ages 8 to 17, who received free 10-minute airplane rides Sunday at the municipal airport open house.* Way to go Shawna!

Even though this is skipping a few years I want to bring in Abby Christina who was born on June 23, 1989. She was confirmed on May 16, 2004, and graduated from Kettle Moraine Lutheran High School, June 1, 2008, as Salutatorian.

Joel and I made a speedy trip down to meet my third granddaughter especially since Joel would soon be leaving on a trip to Washington and he was chosen to be her godfather.

Melvina with all her grandaughters

Shawna, Abby, Jennie
Melvina
Clair
&
2 Cakes!

We were overjoyed with the addition of a third beautiful daughter to the Mehlberg family.

Something special from Abby's early years: From the West Bend paper: "When Abby was in the 2nd grade and 8 years old there is a nice picture entitled "GO BABY GO" showing her blowing a little wooden boat across the channel of water making her winner of the race. That's really something special. It's an adorable picture!

I want to add that we made it to Wisconsin for all of the baptisms, confirmations and graduations. Many a festive meal has been enjoyed at Sarah and Ron's home over the years celebrating these special events.

Joel graduated from Bethany College in 1985. For at least one summer he worked for Jim Schmidt, a well-known landscaper in the Mankato area, and learned a lot about the "tricks of the trade" from him. He took on the project of landscaping our new home. I know he ordered 10 tons of river rock which got dumped at the end of our driveway. I thought this was way too much but he used every bit of it. He planted various kinds of bushes, lots of hostas and whatever was needed to complete the job. It has stood the test of time and I am very proud of the job he did. I know for a while he wanted to put up a split rail fence but I guess he couldn't quite talk his mother into it.

Following his graduation from Bethany College he entered the **University of Minnesota and graduated from there in 1988 with a Bachelor of Science Degree in Business.** I know I wasn't in attendance at the graduation since he

didn't think it was necessary and he did not even participate in it. I know a lot of work went into getting that degree and it has proven invaluable to him. We had a graduation party in our garage, keg of beer and all, of course. I
know he was a little apprehensive about the kind of beer I
would order so I let him choose. He remembers that two
of his favorite Bethany professors, Dean Shoop and Dan
Metzger, were in attendance at his party.

For several years he worked at a Sherwin Williams Auto
Paint store but being in contact with the fumes from auto
paint was not a healthy atmosphere. Thankfully he got
out of there.

 I need to add here that he took a trip to Washington (Aaberg Country) in the summer of 1989. He stayed with
Uncle Paul and Aunt Bea for a few weeks while looking for
employment out there. It just didn't seem like the right fit
and he surprised us by coming back to Minnesota. The
family was all happy to have him back close to home. A lot
of good things happened in the years following.

Teddy **graduated from Harvard University on June 9,
1988,** being awarded the **Degree of Masters of Theology
in Ethics.** His graduation was attended by Mom, Marie, and Uncle Joe. I remember how happy I was when I
caught a glimpse of Teddy marching in with the long line
of graduates. It was the culmination of years of hard work
and dedication.

I remember that we had trouble finding the location on
Harvard Yard where the graduation was to take place.

Uncle Joe thought he knew the exact direction we should go but it was evident that the students wearing caps and gowns were walking in the opposite direction. We finally convinced Joe that we should turn around. And so we did and ended up on what I believe were the library steps. We sat there to get a better view. It was an overcast day with a possibility of rain, and rain it did. People were wearing garbage bags and whatever else they could wrap around themselves to try and keep dry. So much for putting a lot of thought into your outfit for the day. There was a canopy directly overhead which happened to develop a small hole and that gave way to a much larger hole. You guessed it, some people directly under really got a cold river of water down their backs. But it took more than rain to dampen our enthusiasm on such a day as this. The commencement speaker was the President of Costa Rica.

The graduation lunch was served back by the Divinity School. There we enjoyed box lunches, something I had never had before. They consisted of a croissant with a choice of chicken or tuna salad filling, a large brownie like I had never tasted before, and also an apple. What did we have to drink? Was it champagne? Yes!

In the early afternoon a short program for the graduates of the Divinity School was held under a tent, of course. Each of the graduates was recognized and came forward with a statement of what he wanted to pursue. It was pouring down rain. Marie and I didn't quite make it under the canopy for seating and I remember as my umbrella opened up it almost removed the hat of the man seated in front of me.

I don't remember how many days we were there but Teddy drove us around the Boston area quite a bit in his Honda. One evening we had dinner at one of the fancier restaurants in the North End of Boston. They are famous for their excellent restaurants. I was surprised to see the little packets of butter had come from New Ulm, Minnesota. I was also surprised to see a rat run down a sewer hole when we left the building. I learned it is not unusual but you take it in stride. The restaurant was perfectly wonderful. We were pleased that Teddy was able to find dorm rooms where Marie and I stayed overnight. The last night we stayed at a motel which provided transportation to the airport. Uncle Joe bunked at Ted's apartment as he usually did on his many visits to Boston.

This afternoon I am going to attempt to carry on with Ted's employment on the Harvard Campus. I know that he worked part-time in the library at the Divinity School while attending school there, library work being one of his specialties from way back. But the first place that comes to mind is the Kennedy School of Government working under Dennis F. Thompson, author of *Ethics In Congress*, 1995. Marie and I were privileged to meet Mr. Thompson on one of our visits to Boston. He had good things to say about Ted's expertise and research connections, commenting that he knew people from all over the country. His years there were very productive and brought him in contact with a lot of people in important positions which became very helpful in later years. He has become well known for his expertise in research.

On July 5, 1990, we were home at 1208 Adams Street when we received word that Teddy had a cardiac arrest and was hospitalized at Boston City Hospital. Sarah and Ron were here as well as Bill and Christine McCorquodale. You can imagine how shocked we all were to get such news. Immediately we, (Marie and I) made plans to fly out to Boston the next morning. I remember our good friends, Lee and Becky Olson, whom we could always count on to help in any emergency, had cash available for us and also drove us to the airport early the next morning. There were calls made to the hospital where we got some more information, but it was most urgent that we get there as quickly as possible. He had been playing softball with his buddies when he went down suddenly with no earlier symptoms. Fortunately there was a medical student nearby who came and administered life-saving CPR. There was also an off-duty emergency vehicle parked alongside the road so he was taken immediately to Boston City Hospital. It is quite unusual that a person survives a cardiac arrest if those life saving techniques aren't applied immediately. His guardian angel was taking care of him.

When we arrived at the Boston airport an attendant notified us that Paul Chamberlin, a good friend of Teddy's and ours, had made reservations for us at the Howard Johnson Motel which was close by. We stopped there briefly and then took a cab to Boston City Hospital. It wasn't long before Joel and Jon also flew out. It sticks in my memory how Teddy's eyes just bugged out when he woke up and saw us all standing around his bed. The doctors were very well qualified to handle a situation such as this. They wanted to keep him there but when Teddy's boss, Dennis

Thompson, found out about it he contacted his medical friends which included Dr. Linda Emmanuel. [7]   She
insisted that we get him to Mass General Hospital. I am
sure that he would have gotten good care where he was
but we trusted her advice. I am glad we did because he has
received excellent care there all these years. That's twenty
years ago now and he continues to enjoy good health and
has accomplished much in his life.

For several years he enjoyed working at the Harvard
Alumni Law Office in Research and Development. We
were very impressed to be able to visit and meet his co-
workers, Flynn and Toni, as we came to know them. The
Law Office is situated right in the heart of the retail area
around Harvard Square. Shopping at Harvard Square
and the Harvard Coop is a must. I remember how much
I enjoyed going to the Au Bon Pain for lunch and having
a raspberry croissant.

Update: Nov. 13, 2010. He was laid off from his position
at the Alumni Law Office, something that was happening
to many employees across America during the Economic
Crisis. He was awarded excellent benefits plus he left with
very good credentials. Soon he was working part-time at
the Boston University, then at the Harvard Ed School and
now back at the Alumni Law Office on a part-time basis.
He was happy to get back to his friends there but keeping
on a part-time basis seems to be the way to go right now.
This time he is in his boss's office ☺. His former boss was
burned out having been saddled with the whole load and

---

7   At that time Dr. Linda Emanuel was sister-in-law of Rahm
Emanuel, former Chief of Staff of President Obama, and mayor of
Chicago.

quit. He continues to be busy networking and maintaining contact with the HR Department at Harvard.

Good news from Jonathan

Jonathan worked for many years at the Ben Franklin Store in New Ulm, both while going to school and after. I was always anxious for him to get back into school. You can imagine how happy I was when I came home and found a letter on my kitchen table stating that he had been accepted into the University of Minnesota. It was some of the best news I had received in a long, long time. Years back he had purchased a little blue Honda which he called *Ronda the Honda.* This was his faithful transportation for quite awhile. He had been saving money and living very frugally I know. He found a place to stay at the same apartment where Joel was staying.

Jonathan had a variety of jobs to support himself. He worked at UPS on a night shift for quite awhile when he attended the University of Minnesota. He also worked as tutor for the economics department, helping students with their homework. He did a good job at both places; his co-workers appreciated his talents, and the students were lined up outside his office during his tutoring hours. Those years went by pretty fast and it was nice for Jon and Joel to be together in the cities. Probably one of the last places they shared was near the state capitol. I was able to drive to some of the places where they lived by myself but mostly Marie accompanied me. The last place I remember where Jonathan lived was someplace off Lexington. He had all his possessions crammed into a small room, even his little piano. It was a nice house I remember. He had many friends.

Jonathan graduated from the University of Minnesota College of Liberal Arts on **June 14, 1992,** with two degrees: a **BA Summa Cum Laude in Economics and a BS in Statistics.** How proud we were! Marie and I were there and as is customary a family member is allowed to walk part of the distance leading up to the entrance of the auditorium. Marie was privileged to do that and I watched with pride.

After the ceremony we were invited to a luncheon at one of Jon's friend's house, Tsegaye Shibishi, who was from Ethiopia. It was a special lunch and we enjoyed the party very much.

Of course, we had another party at home in our garage. Notable guests who were invited were Prof. Ames Anderson and his wife Ruth who had been one of Jonathan's piano teachers at DMLC. She was an excellent teacher and I am sure Jon appreciated her training. A longtime friend and former roommate from DMLC, Tim Gustafson, and his wife and family were also here. I remember neighbor Dwight Dumke had a remnant of some blue carpet left over from his garage that he installed in the little entryway right outside the kitchen door. It gave the cement floor a boost and made the entrance to the garage more presentable.

We had a keg of beer - I don't know what kind but the boys will remember since they didn't leave the choice up to me. One thing I do know is I had a friend over at Bethany make tubouleh, (a Lebanese parsley dish? It was something special for the day and I was familiar with it but didn't know how to make it.

In order to pursue his education further he applied to several universities. He received scholarship offers from several of them and chose the University of California at Berkeley. My brother Marvin was still living at the time Jonathan came out to California. I often think of how nice it would have been if he and Jonathan could have spent more time together, but Marvin didn't live that many more years. They both would have enjoyed each other's company. I believe that Marvin drove Jon up to El Cerrito where he was able to rent a room for those years he attended the university. I was able to visit him there a couple of times and was very impressed with the lady and her husband who owned the home. Jon took me to a concert on campus on one of those visits. He took a semester break from Berkeley and attended Harvard University studying under Dr. Amartya Sen.[8]

Jonathan studied Economics in the PhD program at Berkeley with a focus on third world economics and ethics and economics. He left the program, however, after earning his Master's Degree to pursue other varied interests. Since then he has done everything from producing his own music to writing and self-publishing his own writing and the writing of others. Currently he's designing lamps and larger installations (such as a solar skylight chandelier for his favorite café, Old Jerusalem Café, where he also does much of the baking). He also manages and maintains the house

8   Dr. Amaryta Sen, winner of the 1998 Nobel Prize in Economics.

in which he lives. He works for several of his neighborhood shops and is occasionally referred to as "the mayor of
Irving Street." He also works for the Department of Elec-
tions when there's an election, which is quite often in San
Francisco. Of course, I have no idea how he makes ends
meet, but he seems to be happy and living quite well.

Joel sets his sites on becoming a lawyer. I need to mention here that two of his professors from Bethany, Prof.
Dean Shoop and Prof. Dan Metzger, were asked to write
letters of recommendation for him which they were happy
to do. He applied to and was accepted at the University
of North Dakota School of Law. He graduated from there
with a Degree of Juris Doctor on **May 13, 1995.** Marie and I were most certainly there for that. Jonathan was
also there and Gary and Judy Goetzke came up for it. We
had a get-together in honor of the occasion at a restaurant
nearby called the 42nd Street Eatery. Marie and I stayed
with some good friends of ours, Jodi and Dan Schmidt,
who lived near Crookston.

Joel made some close friends whom we met while there,
a classmate Christopher Strandlie and his parents. That
friendship has continued especially with Chris who is now
District Attorney in Cass County. Joel worked for a lawyer in Pine River part-time while attending the university
and got a full-time job there after his graduation. He also
worked part-time at a law firm in Grand Forks his last couple of years at the university.

Of course the big thing now was to pass the Bar of the State
of Minnesota. This after much studying and preparation

he did and was admitted to the Bar of the State of Minnesota at a ceremony sponsored by **The Minnesota Supreme Court and The Minnesota State Bar Association, MSBA, October 27, 1995.** What a day to celebrate that was! Marie and I drove to St. Paul and were there for that very important event. Afterwards we went to a nearby neighborhood restaurant to share the excitement with friends of Joel's who had also passed the bar.

He was still working in Pine River at the time he passed the bar, but it wasn't too long before he left his job at that law firm and moved to St. Paul to pursue employment there. For a while he worked for a company called Empi which makes medical equipment.

This was also a very good move because he met his future wife, Deanna, who was and still is working for Medtronic. I first met Deanna the summer of 1999 when Nancy, Michael, and Sarah Lawrence were visiting from California. Joel had arranged for us to meet Deanna for a picnic at Square Lake near Stillwater, MN. That was the first time I laid eyes on my beautiful future daughter-in-law and I was so thrilled. Joel and Deanna came down to Mankato a few times and Marie and I were also invited to her cozy little home in St. Louis Park for a lovely dinner with her and Joel one evening. I don't think it was too long after that Joel brought her down to Mankato and she was wearing a lovely engagement ring.

I quote from their wedding invitation:

*On February seventeenth Two Thousand
Deanna J. Openhowski
and
Joel C. Aaberg
were married on the Island of St. John
The pleasure of your company is requested
at an informal reception
Phalen Park, East St. Paul, Minnesota
June seventeenth, Two Thousand
Celebration begins at 4:30 p.m.
Buffet / Pig Roast begins at 5:30 p.m.*

It is hard to come up with the words that give due justice to Deanna. She has so many wonderful qualities that make her a good homemaker, wife and mother. And what a great cook! She fits into our family so well and I think we also fit very well into her family. It is lots of fun having an extended family with whom we can get together for family celebrations and we have been invited to do that many times.

It seems very appropriate to put in here the birth of my fourth granddaughter, Clair Nicole, born October 10, 2001. We went up to Fairview Hospital in St. Louis Park the very next day to see her and hold her. I can't tell you how happy Marie and I were! Having a granddaughter within pretty easy driving distance has been such a blessing. She was baptized at Norseland Lutheran Church on December 22, 2001. Pastor Craig Ferkenstad officiated and sponsors were Marie Aaberg, and Melvin and Denise Fick (Denise is a twin sister of Clair's mother, Deanna). In addition Grandmother Carol Harms from Sioux Falls, SD, and Darla and Daryl Wagner (Darla is a sister of Deanna) and family plus the Fick children were also there. On the Aaberg side we invited Signe Olson, Becky and Lee Olson, and Rachel and Willis Anthony. This was especially nice since we had no close relatives here to attend. We put on a luncheon in the church basement following the baptism service. It was a great day – she was baptized in the church where her grandfather Theodore A. Aaberg had been pastor for eight years.[9]

Joel and Deanna built a beautiful new home in East Bethel, Minnesota. They were just ready to move in at the time that Clair was baptized. In fact Deanna's whole family came from Sioux Falls and the Luverne, Minnesota, area to be present at the baptism and from there drove up to the new home on Edison Street NE in East Bethel. It was a very happy occasion.

As I mentioned before, having a granddaughter close by has brought me happiness that is beyond words. Many times I have gone up to stay a week at a time or more. During that time Clair and Gramma have become very close friends. We began making Kringla together when she was only three years old. Now she is a pro at it. She has gotten to be very handy in the kitchen, thanks to her mother who has been so good to teach her and let her help at such a young age. I notice she has been eager to help her daddy with the outside chores as well. Buddy, their dog, has become a good companion.[10]

---

9   Signe Olson was one of Joel's baptismal sponsors along with her husband Harry.
10   I didn't expect to have to put a footnote like this in, but Buddy took off and ran away late summer of 2010. They were all

The move to the new seminary at 6 Browns Court.
When the faculty and the Board of Regents first started talking about building a new seminary in 1995 or '6 I felt a little sad about it because our seminary on 447 North Division Street was only about eighteen years old and it was the one which Dad had such a hand in planning. However, I was soon swept into the enthusiasm of the possibility of a new seminary building. We needed more room and being on the campus with the college there were many things to take into consideration when looking at the whole picture. I am quite sure that "Schwan money" had become more available. At first I remember there was some confrontation with the people who lived farther up on Browns Court. The Bethany tennis courts had to be removed and I think the residents worried there would be rowdiness and a lot more traffic, etc. There were many things they could think of trying to discourage us. However, the synod owned the property and there wasn't too much they could do about it. I don't believe it has hurt them at all. In fact, it probably enhanced their property. The new seminary at 6 Browns Court is a beautiful building and attractively landscaped.

Since Wilhelm Petersen was still seminary president at this time, his office was moved into the spacious seminary president's office at the new location. The synod president, George Orvick, had his office in the building on Division Street, so he also moved into the new space provided for the synod president. The building was sort of divided in

---

out in the yard working and playing around including the neighbors across the road who also had dogs who loved to run and play with Buddy. Before they knew it Buddy was nowhere to be found and their constant calling or searching did not bring him back. It was a sad time for them, especially Clair.

half, the south end was synod offices and the north end was specified as seminary offices, chapel and classrooms. I was still the only secretary and my office was right in the middle dividing the two. It was very attractive and spacious with large windows overlooking the ravine in back. I was thrilled!

Here I was again, secretary to both the seminary president and the synod president. I could see everyone who came in the front door. We had a nice little coffee lounge equipped with microwave, refrigerator, sink, cupboards for dishes, etc. There is a large boardroom for meetings which is now up to snuff with easy access for making conference calls, automatic pull-down panels for slides, very comfortable chairs, etc. I should also add that it is very tastefully decorated. I do not hesitate to say that I have baked many a tasty treat for synod board meetings of all departments. I guess the more important the meeting, or rather, the more important the people attending the meeting, the more was put into the coffee treats. I got to know which ones favored scones and which ones liked kringla. The other day as I was eating noon lunch in the college cafeteria, Dr. Kessel walked by my table and said, *"Melvina, that pecan pie is good but not as good as your scones."* For a while I was even buying those little round paper doilies to put between the coffee cup and the saucer. I learned that little bit of "class" from my good friend Delores Fisher, secretary at the college.

However, I don't want to take all the credit for baking treats for meetings. It was about this time that another secretary came on board, part-time at first, in the person of Mary

Jane Tweit. I remember one of the first jobs she got stuck with was helping both Petersen and Orvick pack up their offices from Division Street–packing books and files and getting all these things back in order in their respective new offices. I don't know what I was busy doing but I don't remember helping much with the packing of books. At first she came in only at times when I needed help, but it wasn't long before she was also a full-time secretary. We very much enjoyed working together. We ate our lunch at the workspace looking out toward the ravine. We often saw deer and every once in awhile we would see a cardinal or two. We were still on the time sheet while we ate our lunch since we were right there to answer the phone and take care of any business that came up during that time. Mary Jane and I became good friends although we only occasionally see each other now, mostly at church. When we do get together we have a lot of things to catch up on.

It was very enjoyable for me to be a part of us all getting settled in this new building. The Good Shepherd Chapel is a beautiful place of worship. Occasionally I got called into service by accompanying the seminary choir on the piano when they practiced in the chapel.[11] Not only that but some of the board meetings opened with a devotion service where I was also called into service as pianist. If I ever had any hidden talents, be they ever so humble, they seemed to find out about them.

---

11   One Sunday while I was sitting in Bible Class before second service the director of the Seminary Choir came up to me and said, *"Melvina, we are supposed to sing at 2nd service and we don't have a pianist, could you do that for us?"* It wasn't a difficult piece and so I agreed. I felt so proud when I marched out of there behind the choir.

At this time Wilhelm Petersen was retiring after 17 years of being seminary president so calling a new president by the Board of Regents was on the table. Lots of important decisions were in the works. Congregations were allowed to give their input as to who they felt would make a good president. As it turned out it got down to two men who were being considered. I can still remember how tense I was when the Board was meeting behind closed doors. We didn't bother about going in with coffee or anything at a time like that. I say "we" because Mary Jane was also a full-time secretary. We knew Gaylin Schmeling was one of the candidates and we both felt he was the best qualified. There was a lot on the line because the new seminary president would be our new boss. After much deliberation on the part of the Board and much praying and agonizing on our part the verdict came out – Gaylin Schmeling was called to be the new seminary president.

The new seminary building was dedicated on Synod Sunday at 2:30 in the afternoon, June 15, 1997. New seminary president, Gaylin Schmeling, was installed that same evening at 7 PM.

George Orvick continued to be synod president until 2002 and I was primarily his secretary although during the transition I continued to also serve as seminary secretary. As Mary Jane became more acquainted with her position she took on most of the work of seminary secretary working for Gaylin Schmeling. As I had done before – teaching some of the computer skills that I had learned, I now was privileged to teach Mary Jane. It wasn't long before she became very proficient on the computer and did all the programs, brochures, and would tackle whatever came her way. She got to be very "computer savvy." As I said before, we got to be extremely good friends. We would often joke about how we would settle synod problems thinking we had the best solution. And sometimes I think we did ☺.

For several years we celebrated birthdays of the professors and staff. This was always fun. Sometimes a spouse of the birthday person would send in a cake or some other treat otherwise Mary Jane and I would make sure we had something to serve. One thing I particularly remember was the singing of *Happy Birthday* to the honored guest. The group, being such great singers, picked up the harmony and it was beautiful – Juul Madson's voice had a lot to do with that. Later that practice was stopped; probably it was a good thing since it did take a lot of time and there were a lot of birthdays to celebrate. We always got a card to pass around for everyone to sign, and I guess it was just nice while it lasted. As is often said, *"All good things must come to an end."*

President Orvick retired from the ELS presidency in the summer of 2002. During this time the house right next to the Seminary at 4 Browns Court was being remodeled and turned into the Ottesen Museum with room for other synod offices. George Orvick now became the Director of the Museum and Archives, a job much less demanding than the presidency. He worked it out with the Trustees so that I could have a part-time job as his secretary there when I was ready to retire from my position with the synod/seminary offices. I was very pleased about this. However, I was not ready to move over just yet.

New President of the ELS

John Moldstad succeeded George Orvick as the new ELS president and asked me to stay on as his secretary to help him during the transition.[12] So now I was working for the "new" president of the ELS. I was happy to be asked to do this because I loved my job and I was getting some great benefits including health insurance and a pretty good paycheck each month. I was doing well and I think Dad would have been proud of me.[13] It was a help to John Moldstad since he was new man on the job and I had become well acquainted with the affairs of that office. I thoroughly enjoyed working for him. A big plus for President Moldstad – he was very computer savvy and did a lot of his own letter writing as well as keeping important synod reports and records on his computer. This reduced the large quantity of paper documents which used to fill up the filing cabinets. The work of filing was cut way back and my job was much easier. I used to have a major part in putting out the monthly President's Newsletter to pastors but John really took that over and spruced it up with pictures, kept track of the news that went into it, and to this day gets it sent out at the beginning of each month to nearly all of the pastors, board members and many others by way of the internet. I just can't say enough to compliment John Moldstad. He is a fine Christian leader in all respects and totally committed to keeping the Evangelical Lutheran Synod on a sound scriptural foundation. I was honored to serve as his secre-

---

12   In 1987 I began working as G. Orvick's secretary and continued in that position until he retired from the presidency of the ELS in 2002.

13   I was able to do some updating around my home, new furnace, new air conditioner, new carpeting, papering, painting, etc., and not being so tight with money was a good feeling.

tary for a couple of years. When I walk by his office just to say "*Hi*" he often invites me to come in and gives me a little update on synod affairs. It makes me feel important ☺.

He and his wife, Joslyn, have always generously included me in "happy hours" at their home when they entertain the Trustees once a year and also in the dinners out afterwards at some nice restaurant downtown. This always makes me feel that I am still a part, especially the fun part, of the working group.

At this point I want to make note of the fact that I served as President Wilhelm Petersen's secretary for 17 years which accounts for the total time he was privileged to hold that important office. He was a good teacher and writer and I learned a lot from typing his papers. One of his specialties was *Law and Gospel,* a topic which he was called upon to present many times, either in person or in writing. One of the days after his retirement he called me down to his office and told me he wanted to leave a *legacy* comprised of several papers and sermons he had written over the years. Then he looked at me and said, " *I need a typist.*" This was one of the easier jobs I took on since most of his papers and sermons had already been typed by me and were on my computer. We put out a nice booklet entitled _A Brief Legacy_ which he was able to distribute to his fellow coworkers, certain pastors, family, friends, relatives and to whomever he felt a special kinship.

Now I will devote a few paragraphs about Seminary President Gaylin Schmeling. As I mentioned earlier I was really pulling (praying) for him to get to be the next seminary president. His qualifications were and are exceptional. I characterize him as being one of the hardest working and best-organized individuals I have ever known. In addition to being an excellent teacher and leader he has published many books and papers on various religious and historical topics. Most of them have been written while he has been in the president's office where he has carried a full workload of teaching, preaching and administration. He is also editor of the Lutheran Synod Quarterly. A big burden rests on his shoulders when it comes time to find parishes for the 3rd year students to fulfill their vicarage year and also find parishes for the graduating seniors who are ready to receive a Call into the ministry.

Under his supervision the seminary building is always kept in good order. If repairs are needed he makes sure they get done. The students have a dress code which they follow when school is in session. At functions like the Reformation Lectures or other occasions where they are called upon to serve or whenever they are representing the seminary, they show up in their very best and are a smart looking bunch of guys! I am so proud of them.

It is my pleasure to write a little paragraph about the *First Lady* of the Seminary, Rebecca Schmeling. Becky takes charge of all the decorating of the building for Christmas and Easter. The seminary students are put into service during one of their morning breaks early in December decorating the Christmas tree and helping in whatever way they can under Becky's careful supervision. The same goes for Easter when the wooden cross goes up draped with the proper paramount for the season. She has hosted many great parties at her home or on the seminary grounds, weather permitting. I always look forward to these festivities and have been able to attend almost all of them. The Christmas Party at the Schmelings is one of the highlights of the year. A *Becky Schmeling Party* is really special ☺.

Moving over to the Ottesen Museum

It must have been late in the year 2004 when I really retired from my position and moved over to the Ottesen Museum as part-time secretary to George Orvick. I had a nice office there just as you enter the building. So I was sort of receptionist as well. Home Mission and Foreign Mission meetings were held in the conference room so again I took charge of making sure they had what they needed by way of refreshments. Of course I usually brought in something home baked. My scones, (original recipe coming from Ted in Boston) became a great favorite of theirs.

I was only part-time now so I didn't work every day. I usually came in when I was needed. That got to be quite often since George Orvick decided to put out a book of sermons entitled Forget Not All His Benefits, as his (legacy) to the synod. It got to be a 300 page hardbound book when finished, and I can say that I typed every word of it, this time on the computer, of course.

On December 15, 2010, George and Ruth Orvick left their home base in Mankato and returned to Madison, Wisconsin, where they have two sons and a daughter and other family members living. It was kind of a sad time and I felt a little lonely when I first walked into the office that had been his in the Ottesen Museum since I had also been a part-time secretary for him in recent years. But with age creeping up on them and certain health issues it was important to live near family who could easily be called upon for help as needed.

Archives: Rev. Paul Madson became the full-time archivist after the retirement of W. G. Gullixson and Norman Holte. For a short time his brother Norman Madson was hired to work in the archives as the person to enter records into the computer. However, since at that time he was often called away to fill in for congregations which were without a pastor for quite a lengthy spell, Pres. Orvick asked if I would be willing to work some hours there. At this time I was also working as part-time secretary to Pres. Orvick in the Ottesen Museum but that work was no longer pressing, and I very happily accepted the offer and began my work in the archives Monday, Wednesday and Friday mornings.

The archivist oversees the whole operation, keeping files and boxes in order so information can easily be accessed and stored in its proper place. All the material that comes in needs to be looked over and a decision made as to its value for the archives. Usually most of it is kept and then comes the job of putting it (especially the correspondence) in chronological order, entering the information in a notebook and recording the data that identifies each one. I take it from there and enter the information into the computer.
I need to add here that the first computer we had in the archives I did not really like since I wasn't familiar with it. When it went on the blink I told the worker from the IT Dept. at Bethany that I hoped it couldn't be fixed so we

could get an Apple. He said, "*You may get your wish, and I did.*"

We receive requests for information by email, regular mail, phone, a personal visit or sometimes a note slipped under the door. I need to mention that some requests require quite a bit of research, but that is part of the job and I would say gets to be very interesting sometimes. It is always rewarding to find information that helps someone with his or her family history or fills in some gaps that may be missing in a congregation's church records. The archivist makes sure the humidity is controlled in the inner room where all the important documents are kept.

The work place is very pleasant. Since we are located in the basement of the seminary building we get to know the seminary students quite well and occasionally visitors stop by - sometimes with requests or just to visit. We always have the MN Public Radio music on. I guess we have a couple of complaints though – it gets pretty chilly down there sometimes (we need to dress warmly) and we don't have a phone anymore which is kind of a problem. We share a phone with the library. It's these economic times.

When I retired from being full-time secretary and moved over to the Ottesen Museum I thought that was where I would be working part-time as long as I was able. But getting the job of working in the Archives has been so enjoyable especially since much of it I have become familiar with over my 28 plus years as secretary in the seminary and synod. There are benefits here too – good benefits – I can eat at the college cafeteria for $2.25 a meal, a very good meal. I can go to the concerts at no charge which would normally cost $5.00, thanks to Lois Jaeger our Fine Arts Director over at the Ylvisaker Fine Arts Center.

Tor Jakob Welde was a student who came from Norway with his wife Reiko and little daughter Miriam in 1999. He went through the three-year training program at our seminary. I suppose especially since he came from Norway, but not just that, he and his family are so special to my family and to me. We became very close during those years – I would often go down to the library and visit him a little while he was studying. I learned a lot from him about food in Norway, how you could shred, (he used a Norwegian word which sounded like riffling) apples into your oatmeal and it would taste so good and be so healthy for you. I tried it and it is good. I told him I knew how to make lefse. "*In Norway we buy it,*" he said. So, of course, I had to show them how I made it myself. I take credit for teaching them how to make lefse, and I understand they have my recipe framed and hanging on the wall in their kitchen. I think I sent them one of those potato ricers which are so necessary in preparing the potatoes for lefse making.

When they came to the US in 1999, Miriam was only three years old. She was quite shy at first and remained somewhat shy which is very becoming to a young girl and adds to her fine personality. She began taking violin lessons from the Suzuki School of Music in Mankato when she was five years old. As the time was drawing near for them to return to Norway I asked Miriam to play a piece for me on her little violin. The only way she consented to do this was by hiding behind the big chair in our family room. At the age of nine she performed as guest violinist with the Bergen Philharmonic Orchestra for their 2006 New Year's Concert. By this writing in 2010 she has become an exceptional violinist and is a rising star in her home country of Norway, as well as in Japan, the home country of her mother, where she did extensive traveling as soloist with the Bergen Youth Symphony in the spring of 2010. Now I happily add that she and her parents will be coming to America this coming October and Miriam[14] will be presenting a concert at Bethany Lutheran College. I can't tell you how happy and excited I was to hear that. Everyone I tell this important news to feels as I do. They want to get it on their calendar. I will be privileged to have them as my houseguests for part of their stay here.

In 2006 Marie took me on a two-week trip to Norway. We were so blessed to be able to stay at the home of Tor, Reiko and Miriam. They met us at the Bergen airport and took care of us from that moment on. They have a lovely home with a view of Mt. Ulrik from their balcony. Our very first excursion was a visit to this mountain. We went by cable car to the top. It was fantastic! There was a grand piano way up there in one of the restaurants and Tor, accomplished musician that he is, played for us. I believe it was *Seterjentens Söndag*. Several times at their home we also were entertained by Miriam's violin playing while her father accompanied her on the piano.

Reiko is gifted in many areas, one of them being fluent in three languages: her native tongue Japanese, Norwegian and English. She is also a fantastic cook! Having guests for

---

14   Miriam's official name as it appears on her CDs is *Sonoko Miriam Shimano Welde*.

several days is not an easy job but she came up with one great meal after another and often surprised us between meals with watermelon or other delightful treats. She also works at times for a Japanese theatre production company, helping them prepare tours in Scandinavia and Europe as well as translating, writing, negotiating contracts, etc.

On the weekend we accompanied Tor and family by car and ferry to Avaldsnes where he preached for the Sunday services. We were able to partake of the Lord's Supper with the congregation that Sunday. He is a very dedicated and compassionate pastor preaching the Law and Gospel to the congregations at Avaldsnes and Stavangar. We know there are a lot of other duties that such a faithful pastor as Tor Jakob does in addition to preaching.

While we were at Avaldsnes we were guests at the lovely home of Tor's parents, Odd and Turid, and were treated royally. Turid made some very special Norwegian meals and treats for us and set a most beautiful table, together with the help of her husband Odd. I just can't find words that due justice to our trip and stay with Tor, Reiko, Miriam and also his parents. They took us to some very special museums as well as other well-known Norwegian places of interest. We also were privileged to have coffee at the home of Tor's grandmother, Lydia,[15] and also visited the home of his maternal grandmother where we met other relatives.

Before we left Norway Tor took us on a two-day trip to "Aaberg Country" and that was Sogndal. We saw the name

---

15   Lydia passed away in 2010. In my curio I have a pair of Norwegian dolls dressed in beautiful holiday costumes which she made for me. They are a real treasure.

Aaberg around there quite often. At the end of my journal I have added copies of my annual Christmas letters.[16]

Marie's Career Change

Marie was honored at Mt. Olive on May 5, 2002, in recognition of her 25 years of service as a Christian Day School teacher in our synod. It was a lovely event and time to reminisce about her teaching years at Saude, Scarville, and Mt. Olive. More than once I have heard someone say she was one of the best teachers Mt. Olive ever had. That's quite a testimony!

It had been a goal of hers to take a one-year sabbatical after completing 25 years of teaching and do a year of volunteer work at Mayo Clinic in Rochester. She wanted to do it out of gratitude for the excellent care her Dad received and also for the exceptional care I received when I had open-heart surgery there in 1999. During the 2002-2003 school year, she took an unpaid sabbatical and tried something new by volunteering as a Surgical Messenger at Saint Marys Hospital in Rochester. Through hard work and planning she was able to make "ends meet" during that year when she wasn't on any payroll. It was a very fulfilling and inspiring experience.

She returned to teaching at Mt. Olive the next school year. As much as she enjoyed teaching all those years, it seemed God was leading her in a new way to serve. She appreciated the many people who supported her in this decision to look at a new way to use her talents. In February 2004, she was contacted by the coordinator of the Saint Marys Hospital Volunteer Program that a new program for students

16   Check my 2006 Christmas letter.

was being established, and a job posting was open for applicants. After going through some very intense interviewing, she was offered the position to be Coordinator of the Mayo Clinic Young Volunteers. She accepted and began working at Mayo Clinic on July 6, 2004.

Mt. Olive expressed their appreciation for Marie's 20 years of teaching there by hosting a farewell. She appreciated the many thoughtful words expressed and especially remembers the kind words which Juul Madson wrote, "*May God bless you in your new role as His able ambassador.*" It has turned out to be a new and wonderful career. Lots of hard work to be sure but she has made that program grow beyond all expectations and gained the highest respect of her colleagues. The Appreciation Night events that she plans for her volunteers reflect the many features of the program and the volunteers' contributions. I have been privileged to attend two of these Appreciation Night banquets and I hear many good things about Marie and how the Young Volunteer Program has thrived under her supervision.

TRIPS: Marie and I are good traveling companions. We have been on many trips together, most of them were the result of Marie's generosity picking up the tab for the tickets. I don't remember the order of the early trips but that doesn't really matter. We went to Washington, D.C. and rented a room at the home of Sennie Granger who lived only six blocks from the capitol. We took in the Fourth of July celebration on the lawn of the nation's capitol. It didn't take long for us to find our way around the city by using the metro rail. You can get almost any place you want to go if you have a good map and schedule for their modes of transportation. We took in places like the Library of Congress where we were able to request a copy of Dad's book, "*A City Set on a Hill*," published in 1968. We felt proud to be looking in the card catalog of this famous library and find it noted there. Other places toured were the Smithsonian, the Federal Bureau of Investigation, the Treasury Building, the White House, the Supreme Court Building, the U. S. Capitol, and the National Rifle Range (We did this for Joel). We must have picked up a brochure from there. I remember one time we went to a McDonalds for lunch and found we were the only white people in there. Quite often we picked up food at a grocery store and made do that way.

Hawaii: I had never thought of getting to Hawaii but Marie had been there with her good friend Becky Olson, and she wanted to make sure I got to go there, too. She took me there to celebrate my 65th birthday in July of 1991. We stayed on the island of Maui. You can imagine what a fantastic time we had! It was the first time I had been off the mainland of America.

Marie and I ventured to Norway in 1997 to visit the land of our forefathers. Norway is the very best of places to travel. We took a tour of the country by bus for the first week and then on to Lillehammer and Kvam where my grandmother Oline and my great grandfather Johannas Bakken had lived. The *stabur* was still in use – a place where they kept their supply of flatbread for the winter. After losing his wife, Johannes immigrated to America with his three children, Oline, Annie, and Albert. Someone else, probably Teddy, will do some more extensive research into the history of our relatives immigrating to this country.[17]

Several times I have been to Boston – some of these are mentioned earlier in my writings or in my Christmas letters. Mostly I have had Marie with me, but sometimes I have traveled alone. One year Sarah came out and a special memory I have of that trip was when Teddy took us to the patriotic concert put on by the Boston Pops in their famous auditorium on Flag Day. The featured guest soloist was Daniel Rodriguez, the policeman who became famous after the memorial service of the terrorist attack on the World Trade Towers on 9/11. I play his CD often when I am working around the house. It makes my housework go along so much easier.

Trips to Tracy – There have been numerous trips to Tracy over the years to visit and stay in touch with relatives there. These trips have gotten fewer, but when family comes from California and time is really busy on the farm we make a call and arrange to meet at the Red Rooster for coffee. We can catch up on a lot of news in a short time. Marie and I just attended the 125th anniversary of the town of Garvin, a great event, and Buzzy and Barb were on the planning committee. We also visited Bernetta at the Prairie View Nursing Home in Tracy. It has always been such fun over the years to go to Buzzy and Barb's family celebrations: confirmations, graduations, and weddings. Being in fairly close driving distance has been a good thing!

---

17   For more information check my 1997 Christmas Letter.

Special Events

The year 2008 was a very important year for Norseland. It was the Sesquicentennial (150 year anniversary) of Norseland Ev. Lutheran Church. I remember when word came out about the celebration, I passed the news around to you children and you were as excited about it as I was. It made me very happy that you all were there to take part in that celebration. Dad was pastor there from August 1968 until August 1976 and I taught Christian Day School there from 1947 – 1950. We lived there as a family for eight years.

Trip to California, July 21 – 31, 2010   Teddy took me on a ten-day trip to California. It was a wonderful vacation visiting our many relatives there. Here's a little background on the California connection. My brother Marvin had left Minnesota and decided to make California his home soon after he graduated from high school. He was my only brother who graduated from high school. He was blessed with a talent for building as well as running a business and getting along with people. My Uncle Clarence, my mother's brother, and his family had moved there earlier as did my Aunt Emma and her family. So he wasn't without family when he moved out West. Then along came World War II and he joined the Navy. I remember how I worried about him. When he was home on furlough I couldn't hold back the tears when he was ready to leave again. The same went for Orlando who enlisted in the army and served in the Signal Corps. After the war Marvin met his wife Terry whose memory I hold dearly. He developed a very successful business over the years. I need to comment here about the close relationship I enjoy with my nieces, Christine and Nancy. They have been like daughters to me and have remembered me in so many special ways over the years. That also includes their families.

Since we have very close family there we have traveled to California many times over the years, and since Jonathan has also left the Midwest and taken up roots in California it is an even more compelling desire to visit there.

The trip in 2010 was especially wonderful. We spent special time with nieces Christine and Nancy and their families, visited Yosemite National Park, and also visited good friends Phil Lawrence and his wife Barbara. Our home base was Jonathan's apartment located near the Golden Gate Park. We got to know Jonathan's close friends in the neighborhood. Even though San Francisco is a very large city, each neighborhood has its own special interests and many of the people there enjoy a special bond. Walking along the street with Jonathan that is very evident.

Here I can't leave without telling about the Old Jerusalem Café where we went for coffee and lunch nearly every day we were in the area. It was so great and I think about it nearly every day as well as the shop owners who make it extra special. Since Jonathan returned to California after his Christmas in Minnesota he is helping out there by baking some of his specialties: scones, Clementine cake, and muffins. His latest undertaking is being the weekend bread baker making baguettes. I can't wait to have him bake some for me while he is home. It sounds as though he has really perfected the recipe. I was talking with a good friend of mine the other day and when I told him about Jon's bread baking for the Old Jerusalem Café he said, "*I am never surprised when you tell me about anything that Jonathan can do.*"

Bastet's Kindle is another little shop where I loved to look around, and it's only a few steps from Jon's front door. I came home with many gifts of jewelry from this place and a set of very small cups and saucers from the estate of Paloma Picasso, daughter of the famous artist Pablo Picasso. Jonathan has helped the store owners of Bastet's Kindle with chores of all kinds and has earned a lot of credit there. It was largely through Jonathan's generosity helping out there that I came home laden with so many beautiful gifts. He also has his creation of "*Will o' the Wisps*" on sale in that shop. I came home with four of them. If the solar bulb gets some sunshine during the day it will light up at night. This is one of Jon's designs and they are so beautiful. [18]

Trip to Ft. Myers and Doral/Miami, FL

Just when I thought there were no more trips on the horizon for me, Marie came up with the idea that we should fly to Florida over Easter to visit my granddaughters (her nieces), Jennie and Shawna. Thanks to Shawna, we were able to locate some pretty reasonable tickets. She could be a travel agent if she ever decides to quit teaching.

We flew from Rochester to Ft. Myers where Jennie picked us up on the Thursday before Easter. It was wonderful to see where she has been living and teaching for the past nearly four years. Their layout for school and church is very

18 Check my 2010 Christmas Letter for more details about the California trip.

spacious and beautiful. Jennie showed us all around her school and we took her picture while she stood outside her office door under the sign that said: DIRECTOR. We were able to attend services at Crown of Life Lutheran Church for both Good Friday and Easter Sunday and also enjoyed their Easter Brunch. I would like to duplicate some of the things they served for their brunch sometime, but I would need a few recipes. Jennie took us to Lakes Park to see the beautiful flowers and flowering trees in bloom. One particular tree was called the Shaving Bush Tree; it was large with pink blossoms that were shaped like a shaving brush, so I thought it should have been called that – but it wasn't. It was spectacular as were many other flowers and trees. Jennie drove us to Shawna's in Doral by way of Alligator Alley (they call it that since alligators are swimming in the ditches along the road.) You don't want to have car trouble there. The highway is very good but absolutely nothing to see along the highway except swampland.

Shawna drove us to downtown Miami that evening. Even though the traffic was crazy she just swung through that with no problem at all. It was great to see the tall buildings, all the lights, the beautiful Atlantic Ocean, the ships, and view the famous sites as she pointed them out to us. After some driving around we found a place to park and enjoyed our pizza dinner outside at one of the restaurants on the main strip where a lot of other establishments were also serving outdoors.

Next day Shawna packed a delicious picnic lunch and drove us to Miami Beach, and again the traffic was very heavy but no problem. We enjoyed sitting under a large umbrella by the ocean. Jennie and Shawna were working more on their tan. Of course we wanted to see where Shawna taught school, Divine Savior Academy, before our return trip to Ft. Myers. That is really a huge establishment. I was very impressed and she is, no doubt, doing a great job there.

The Monday after Easter was a free day for Jennie and we were able to get over to the orange juice place where you can have all you want to drink. Since drinking their mixture of *Orange Juice* and *Cranberry Juice*, I mix that drink for myself at the college cafeteria now every day. I had never tried it before and it is delicious. We also got our shopping in so we could come home with something special from Florida.

I have been on many trips these years:

Washington DC
Hawaii
Kansas
Boston many times
California many times
New York in connection with Ted's graduation
from Princeton
Norway in 1997
Norway in 2006
California in 2010
Florida in 2011

"Gramma Time with Clair"[19] 2005

Joel and Deanna had been married for five years on February 17, 2005, and to commemorate this event they took a trip to Mexico. This made it necessary to find someone to stay at home and take care of Clair. That February 21st Joel drove down to Mankato after work at Medtronic to pick me up. We enjoyed supper at the Tav on the Ave before heading back. He and Deanna were leaving early in the morning on Wednesday, February 23rd. So began my stay-watching granddaughter Clair, age 3 years and 4 months. The first morning I had my clock set for 7 a.m. (Clair's usual wake up time) and when I opened my eyes there she was sitting out in the hall outside her parents' bedroom waiting for Gramma to wake up. We both hopped into the big king sized bed and I started looking for cartoons on the TV they have in their bedroom. After trying a few channel's with no luck Clair looked at me and said, "We need cartoons, don't we Gramma?" After a few tries we found some. Pretty soon, as is the usual morning schedule, we moved downstairs and watched cartoons on the big TV. I went out into the kitchen to get the morning coffee going. I started grinding the coffee and pretty soon I heard, "That's enough now Gramma." Daddy and Clair usually make the coffee in the morning and he has taught her the ins and outs of making really good coffee by not grinding the beans too long.

Since it is her regular routine to go to the Teddy Bear Day Care during the day we kept that up with a modified

---

19   I use the spelling Gramma in my writings about Clair because it sounds so right … just the way she says it. I hear it in my ears ☺.

schedule (I took her in late about 10 a.m. or sometimes 11 and picked her up about 3 or 4 in the afternoon. Each day when I came to pick her up she greeted me by running over and grabbing me around the legs. If she didn't see me right away one of her friends would always say, "Clair, your Gramma's here." If she was watching a movie with the others or playing some other game I asked her if she wanted to stay longer or go home. The answer was always, "I want to go home." She was good at watching the road and telling me which direction to go and when the lights turned from red to green. We always listened to some of her favorite little songs which were on CDs in Deanna's X Terra which I got to drive those days. I should say that it took some doing on some days to get her convinced that she was supposed to go to Day Care. She kept saying, "No, not today." The first day she was running around and hiding from me. She even got the gate open going down the stairs into the lower level of the house and walked down there. Of course, I was right behind her, but she quickly came out from "hiding" and said, *"I heard a scary noise down here."* There was no more going down there by herself for the rest of the week.

Clair was good at remembering where her Mommy and Daddy went – MEXICO, but she never fussed about being left at home with Gramma. The first day she told me they were going to bring her a present and pointed to me and said, "And you too!" Boy, did we have something to look forward to. We talked about that quite a bit.

Before I go any further I should tell about the neat surprises Deanna had for Clair every morning. She made up envelopes for every day of the week they were gone with a card inside telling where she had hidden a surprise for her. That was the first thing we did every morning. They were hidden in places like her box of Lego's, the kitchen mixer, under her bed, in her bathroom, in Clair's closet, in the laundry room, in her big girl panty drawer, and the best hiding place of all which brought the most giggles was Mommy and Daddy's bathtub. She got the biggest kick out of that – something hidden in the bathtub. That really tickled her funny bone. She had lots of fun with her new gifts – painting, drawing, even a new movie one day.

The first day when we were driving into the driveway, Clair said, "*This is my home and my Mommy and Daddy live here with me.*" So I could tell she was thinking about them but she was being a big girl about their being gone for a few days. That first night when it was bedtime I read some stories to her and we sang some songs. Then she was going to play the host and told me to go into the big king sized bed and she followed me in and covered me up and told me to shut my eyes and go to sleep. I didn't think that would last but I went along with her. Soon she came in and said, "How about you rub my back a little bit?" So I got out of bed again and got her tucked in, rubbed her back, said prayers with her, and sang to her until she fell asleep. I didn't hear anything from her until 7 a.m. the next morning, but I had checked on her a couple of times just to make sure she was covered.

The next day, Thursday, we had the same ritual in the morning. I ground the coffee with no remarks coming from Clair. Guess I had caught on. I think I made pancakes for breakfast which she ate with some delicious strawberry jam that Uncle Ted had made last summer. It was a bit of a chore again to talk her into going to Day Care, but we made it. I believe that morning I asked her if she would like spaghetti for supper and she did. Funny thing was when I picked her up from Day Care that afternoon she reminded me that we would be having "buzghetti" for supper. She also got a surprise in the mail that day – a gift from Uncle Ted of 6 beautifully colored Crate and Barrel bowls in different sizes. She used the red one for eating her spaghetti out of that night. It worked really great – those long noodles would just slide up the sides of the bowl into her mouth. She enjoyed a really great supper. We played a lot of house – usually I was the baby and she the mommy, but the roles switched frequently. One day while we were playing house and I was the Mommy she asked, "Would you like a little wine?" We played going to the doctor and going to the dentist. We also played a lot of hide and seek which seems to be a favorite of children. While I was fixing supper Clair said, "We really played hard today, didn't we Gramma?" I readily agreed.

I got acquainted with her favorite shows Cai U and Dragon Tails. It was always easy to get her out of the tub when Cai U was coming on. It didn't take me long to catch on to that. When it comes to baths I need to say this: The last two nights that I was giving her baths she insisted on cold water. She said her favorite water was cold. Of course, she couldn't sit down in it and I did the best I could to get it mixed with a little warm water and we washed very quickly– just trying something different on Gramma I guess.

On Friday evening we anxiously awaited Auntie Rie's arrival from Rochester. After she came Gramma got a break. Marie took the night shift, gave her baths, read books – put her to bed - all kinds of things. One morning before Marie came, Clair found a picture of her and she asked me if Auntie Rie was my best friend. I said *"She's my daughter and also one of my best friends."* She said, *"She's my best friend too."* She can be quite a conversationalist.

On Saturday morning it was time to make a Swedish T–Ring. It was Clair's first time helping with a T–Ring. When I got out the big rolling pin she asked if I had brought the one that was just her size. She remembered this from our lefse-making day at Christmas time. She is a whiz with the rolling pin. And we have pictures to prove it.

On Saturday afternoon we took Clair to a movie. It was Winnie the Pooh . . . very cute and entertaining. Marie and I also enjoyed it. After that we went to the grocery store and Clair, of course, drove the cart and helped us pick up the groceries. At one spot in the dairy section there is a huge life-sized figure of a cow and when you push the button it talks to you. What a hit!

On Sunday early afternoon we went shopping at Target, but before we went we stirred up Kringla. Clair has helped with that many times and is improving with the twist each time. Our shopping trip was lots of fun. Clair, like her Mommy, loves shopping. On our way home there was another quick stop at the grocery store. We bought a pizza for supper. What a good idea! I got started making another T–Ring while Clair and Auntie Rie were busy. When I got it done she said, *"Did you make one without me?"* Shame on Grandma for doing that. Truth was I wanted to get one ready to bring over to the neighbors across the street. John had been so kind to come over and help us with our TV when we got it all goofed up with the remote control. He also blew snow out of the driveway. Clair went with me over there and they invited her to stay and play with Maddie, her friend. That worked out so well. When she was gone I got started on rolling the Kringla but saved some for her to do. We also made another T–Ring which she helped with this time. Oh what fun!

Clair always reminded me that we needed to pray before we ate and she knows the entire two verse prayer *"Come Lord Jesus Be Our Guest"* and says it very well. What a girl!

Marie took Monday off so she was able to stay for 3 days – 3 wonderful days!! On the late afternoon of Monday Clair fell asleep late in the day. We didn't want Aunty Rie to leave while she was sleeping so we tried to wake her up. It wasn't easy but she finally opened her eyes. We were trying to get her to say goodbye and had to give up on that but when Marie drove out of the driveway and I came back in from the garage there she was at the window waving goodbye. She's such a sweetheart.

She loved playing outdoors in the snow and both Gramma and Auntie Rie had her outside for some good old fashioned sledding and making angels in the snow.

One of the songs which I sang for her (I was thinking of every song I could to put her to sleep) was "My Bonnie

Lies over the Ocean." She really liked that and it brought a smile to her face even when she was dozing off. It brought a smile to my face when I heard her singing it in the bathroom one morning. We later realized she was singing "My Body Lies Over the Ocean." Perhaps that has been corrected by now.

Some highlight phrases of Clair's.

- "Does that sound like a good thing to do?"
- "Sure"
- Want some?
- "I need to dance" No matter what she is doing – if one of her shows is coming on and they start with a little dance, she has to get up in front of the TV and dance along. That is so cute.
- She loves giving Barney Hugs too.
- One day while Clair was riding in the car with Gramma and Marie we were talking about people going to college and what they wanted to be. She said, "What did my Daddy want to be – A Daddy? Marie and Gramma both assured her she had it right – he wanted to be a Daddy.

Funny thing – when Mommy and Daddy came home they expected her to come running to them with open arms as she usually does, but she was busy putting clothes on her Barbie doll and didn't turn around when she heard them. Was she putting a guilt trip on them for being gone? Her parents, of course, felt badly but she soon warmed up. They brought her a lovely Mexican dress and another outfit. I got a beautiful painted wooden plate (Joel said it was Mexican rosemaling ☺. It has a beautiful blue background and is covered with yellow flowers. It's gorgeous!

Next morning Deanna took me to Mankato and stopped by the Post Office so I could pick up my mail and also took me to Dunn Brother's Coffee for lunch.

I was home again in my own bed – but during the night I woke up thinking I should check on Clair, but I didn't find any Clair at my house.

Gramma Time with Clair and Chester, 2011

It happened that Clair was on spring vacation from school the first full week of March, 2011. Joel called to see if Gramma could possibly be put into service again, this time not only to watch Clair but also Chester, the new puppy. Spending time with Clair is a very special time for me and I was happy for the opportunity. Joel drove to Mankato to get me on Sunday. While I was finishing our meatloaf and baked potato dinner, he put a new light fixture in the bedroom downstairs and also did a minor repair in the bathroom. While I finished the dishes he went out and cut down part of an apple tree that had fallen during a storm. He can get a lot of chores done in short order.

Now about Chester: He's a cute little puppy, nearly all white but with the promise of some chestnut spots on his face trying to make their appearance. Since it was too cold for him to be outside we took care of him in the family room downstairs. I had never taken care of a puppy before but lucky for me Clair knew all the rules. It was winter with lots of snow still on the ground so Clair was the one in charge of taking him out. I watched from the window. He was getting a little more adventurous with each trip and began to wander a little farther into the woods, but when she called him he came running up the path and followed her back to the house. I had strict orders not to go out. I minded pretty well on that score. Clair was always willing to take him out. You can't read a puppy's mind. If he stands in front of the patio door going out and barks we thought it meant he needed to go out – sometimes it did and sometimes it didn't.

He loved to run upstairs into the kitchen and the living room and even up the next flight of stairs into the bedrooms. We caught on a little too late that we should have those doors closed. He had a pretty big accident in Clair's bedroom one day and also in the living room a couple of times. Clair explained to me just how to take care of that. You take a zip-lock bag and turn it inside out then put your hand in there and you are able to just pick up the mess. She had her chance to put into practice what she had so carefully explained me and I was so proud of her. There are certain rules you have to follow while training a puppy: Don't let him up on the furniture and don't put him in his kennel for punishment. We put him in there sometimes just so we could get a break when we ate our lunch or did some baking and also at night for sleeping, of course. It was so cute to see Chester and Clair take naps together in front of the fireplace. They are very fond of each other and he's a great companion for her.

I need to add that Clair and Gramma baked Clementine cake, Oatmeal Icebox Cookies and Pizzelles that week. We share a special bond when it comes to baking. She is so good at reading a recipe and measuring the ingredients that I feel she really doesn't need much help. She also knows where everything is in the cupboards and the pantry and all about using the big Kitchen Aid mixer. We just don't want her to be alone when using the stove and oven. One day for breakfast she made pancakes for us and they turned out great after we found a non-stick pan ☺.

It was a great diversion from my regular week at home. Deanna is a fantastic cook and can come home from work and put together a really great meal in no time at all. Joel also is very much into meal preparation, grilling, doing meat in the smoker, etc. They make a great pair. Joel and Deanna took us out for dinner a couple of evenings and I also got in on two of Clair's swimming lessons. She's becoming a very good swimmer. Marie came up and enjoyed the latter part of the week with us. She also brought me home which saved Joel a trip.

JENNIE, SHAWNA AND ABBY

Jennifer, Shawna, and Abby, my first three granddaughters have grown up into beautiful, mature, and I must say well-educated adults. Of course they know what they have done, but others who read this may not know so I need to write a few things down. Jennie and Shawna, after completing 5 years at Martin Luther College in New Ulm, Minnesota, are both teaching children in the Early Childhood Programs of their respective churches in Florida. What a blessing they are to all of those little ones who come under their tutelage. Abby is well on her way to becoming a teacher also in the same basic field as her older sisters. They are all very dedicated and use their talents well. Since they lived in Wisconsin all of their lives I have not been able to spend as much time with them as I would have liked.

Both Jennie and Shawna were chosen as dorm parents at Martin Luther College during their final years there. The other day I happened to be at a luncheon where I met the professor who had hired them to this position and he spoke highly about their capabilities.

An update about Jennie: She recently received and accepted a Call from Martin Luther College in New Ulm to be the lead teacher in charge of the Early Childhood Center and supervisor of students who are preparing to go out into the teaching ministry in the Early Childhood Program. This is a program that is growing by leaps and bounds in the Wisconsin Synod and we are so proud of her that she has been chosen to play this important part in that program at the college. She will have completed four years as teacher at Crown of Life Lutheran Church in Ft. Myers, Florida, before beginning on her new venture.

One winter evening during Shawna's final year in college she and her friends came to Mankato to ski. It happened that a bad snowstorm came up making the trip back to New Ulm rather hazardous. Good thinking Shawna called Grandma and asked if I could put up seven people for the night. It was a thrill for me to do that! I quickly got all the beds ready that I could. Everyone got a place to sleep. I think I made hot chocolate and whatever we could put together to eat. It was lots of fun and I got some very special thank you notes from them.

This is news from Shawna of a different nature but very important just the same: The Doral City League Volleyball team that she plays on took the championship. Quite a thrill since the players on the other team were some terrific volleyball players, too.

Realizing there wasn't much time left in the school year I wanted to get in touch with Abby to see if I could work out a lunch date with her and her roommate. Sure enough she was available the very next day, Sunday. While I was walking outside I saw these two gorgeous girls coming out of the dorm. I thought the one girl was a little too tall to be Abby, but pretty soon I heard, "*Hi Grandma.*" Abby, always the fashion plate, was wearing high-heeled shoes. They were definitely cute. Of course her two older sisters know how to be fashionable, too!

This summer, 2011, Abby will be working for the WELS Kingdom Workers in Houston, Texas. She will be using her talents as a teacher to work with the young children in the congregation there. It will be an interesting experience and prove helpful to her in the years to come when she is a full-time teacher in Elementary/Early Childhood Programs of their synod.

It is time for me to be winding down on my Journal writing. I thought it important to update some information on my children. Joel is presently working for a company called

Inspire Medical Systems which makes, of course, medical equipment. Right now they are working on a new method for treating *Sleep Apnea*. He does some traveling in connection with his work, sometimes to Washington, D. C. to meet with the FDA. Deanna and Clair got to accompany him on a business trip to Switzerland. What a treat for the family! This spring, 2011, he was able to spend some time with Ted while on a business trip to Boston. That worked out so well for the brothers to spend a little time together.

I sent Deanna an email asking for information about her job at Medtronic. I know she has an important job there and I wanted to get it right. I quote here: *"I work in the Neuromodulation Division of Medtronic in the Clinical Research Department. I assist with helping manage activities related to clinical study management."* She is also a great cook and in addition to her cooking skills she keeps a beautifully decorated home as well as many gorgeous flowerbeds to adorn the yard. Joel and Deanna work together on keeping their lawn and newly fenced in garden in good shape and they have done many projects around the house. They all enjoy camping and fishing.

And now, last but not least, there is Clair Nicole who will be 10 on October 10 this year. She was born in 10/10/01. So I think that calls for a special celebration this fall. She is a very good student and is in the third grade at Cedar Creek Community School which is located in East Bethel. This school year Joel has worked it out so he can stay home in the morning with Clair until the bus comes. That is really neat since several other parents also come down with their children, and give them a goodbye hug before putting them on the bus. Some bring their coffee cups and if there is time they can chat a little with neighbors. I always like going down to the bus stop with Clair when I am there.

For the past several years we have enjoyed celebrating our family Christmas party at Joel and Deanna's. They are very generous to let us all move into their beautiful home in the north woods for our celebration. Note: Jennie, Shawna and Abby – no more running upstairs to use the bathroom and shower. Joel has finished the bathroom downstairs and without saying more, I will just say it is ELEGANT! When Clair proudly showed it to Marie and me she said, *"My Dad made this all by himself."* She also said this: *"My Dad said this is my LAST project for a LONG time."*

Jonathan is a man of many talents: His talent for music includes composition. My Christmas gift from him in 1988 was his own composition *"Lullaby (Away In A Manger).* It is a beautiful variation of that favorite Christmas Carol. Jonathan has many ways of showing his love. I wish I had known more about my own father. Could it be that Jonathan inherited some of his talents? I never heard that my father played the piano but he bought my mother a piano, the very one I have in my downstairs right now so he must have liked music. I feel he was a very tender-hearted person with a tall and slender build like Jonathan. He was the first one in the community to buy a car and my Aunt Elma's favorite brother. That says a lot.

The Laplander Goose

Another of his talents: He wrote a book! He wrote a beautiful story entitled <u>The Laplander Goose </u>which was copy-righted in 2002. I was privileged to receive the very first hand-bound edition. It is a beautiful book with a beautiful story. I always keep it on my coffee table in the living room where I see it nearly every day and I enjoy showing it to people who come by.

Marie - I have written about her work at the Mayo Clinic as the Coordinator of the Mayo Clinic Young Volunteers. It is almost mind boggling all the work she is able to accomplish. She has some spunk/backbone that I don't have and that is: She can *"run a tight ship."* She gets this from her Dad. She has helped me more than I can say when she comes home weekends – does things around the house, sneaks out and fills my car up with gas, buys groceries, takes care of the lawn, etc. I am amazed at how many things she can fix. This spring she has taken on a major project of getting rid of a lot of stuff around here that is just taking up space in the basement. We love playing Chinese checkers and are pretty evenly matched but I think Marie is gaining on me. Marie, living closest to me, is my constant source of help and encouragement whenever I need it.

Sarah and Ron. Ron is head of the Religion Department at Kettle Moraine Lutheran High School in Wisconsin. He plays an important role in getting young men interested in studying for the ministry. He teaches Latin and Religion, two very important subjects for high school students. I can safely say that my three granddaughters, Jennie, Shawna, and Abby took Latin for all four years from their father. There are a lot of other duties expected of him: He visits congregations in the surrounding area and preaches a "Kettle Moraine Sunday" sermon several times a year. That gets to be a lot of sermon preparation and traveling. He is also one of the track coaches so he is a busy man in the spring of the year.

He also keeps beautiful vegetable and flower gardens, and a well manicured lawn – not to let him get by without mentioning how much he has learned to do in the kitchen by way of baking bread, preparing meals, etc. He's also a good cleaner and a big help to Sarah. Since they are both teaching they get together on the housework.

Sarah taught a large number of piano pupils for eight years before returning to classroom teaching. Having Mrs. Silber as a teacher for several years, she was able to pass on the skills of excellent piano technique to her pupils, and many of them have become good pianists themselves because of her training. At the close of every year she hosted a piano recital for her pupils always ending the recital with Sarah performing one of her favorite piano solos. Refreshments were also served making a very special afternoon complete.

She has been teaching 4th grade at Good Shepherd Lutheran School in West Bend for many years now and has the reputation of being an excellent teacher. She's a great cook, baker and seamstress – I could go on and on. Also she has a chance to make use of her musical talents by playing for weddings – something she did several times this past summer.

On one of her trips to Mankato last fall she put new curtains up in my bedroom. We made a trip to Penney's in the morning, got the material we needed, and with a few instructions from the clerk we were good to go. Sarah made a couple of phone calls to Jon when we had a little trouble making holes with the drill (*first time using a drill*). It turned out we needed different drill bits. Beautiful curtains are the finished product and they are a joy to me every day. She's a busy mother doing good things for her children – sending care packages, sewing, and giving help over the telephone on whatever questions they have.

I have said the Mehlbergs are a *family of teachers;* they are also a *family of shoppers.* When the girls are home they all, (Dad, Mom, and daughters) love going to Milwaukee to shop – even if the time is short they squeeze it in somehow.

My children keep in touch with me often either by phone or email. Teddy calls me nearly every Sunday evening. In fact I just got a call from him a few minutes ago and it's not Sunday, but he had some good news to share about a telephone interview he just had. He has weathered the economic crunch quite well, has developed new hobbies, and gotten to be a very good craftsman. He built a colonial cupboard fashioned just the way they were back in earlier days. It's a beautiful piece of furniture. He made Sarah a Nantucket bench for her birthday. For my Mother's Day gift this year he made a beautiful cherry wood Chinese checkerboard for me. That is almost a tongue twister when I say it. Is anyone up for a game of checkers? He has been able to enjoy playing golf for a big part of the year out in Boston. He also enjoys teaching the sport to a group of 12 boys who have special needs. This past year a boy whom he coaches received a Gold Medal at the Massachusetts Special

Olympics. He gets a couple of good vacations every year and I always enjoy it when he comes home and takes on some projects around the house or garage. I also like it when he cooks for me. Homemade soups are one of his specialties.

On August 20, 2000, I began keeping a Journal by writing down important events in my life and the lives of my family. I was 74 years old at the time and now it is eleven years later. Had I started much earlier and kept good records it would have been easier. Since that didn't happen, I have had to rely on my memory, other people's memories, and the multitude of letters and writings that have been surfacing ever since I began in earnest with this project. I have found so many treasures – letters from my children, writings they have done for class assignments when they were young, and files and boxes of things which meant a lot to me and I had kept over the years. This helped me so much with my research.

When my family told me they planned to celebrate my 85th birthday this year we decided it would be a good time to have my Journal completed. I am sure there could be more to write about but this particular Journal will come to an end. I have other things I would also enjoy doing and it would be a welcome change to take a break from writing.

———·———

As a closing I decided to include this prayer which Dad had written down for our family left behind when we went to Arizona in 1979. (We had hoped that a climate change would be of some benefit for his health, but that did not happen so we returned home.)

Dad's words:

> *"My daily evening prayer for myself, and the second stanza for each of my family: Dr, Franz Pieper said every evening prayer of a Christian must eventually come to this that we tell God that now He is going to have to stay awake because I am going to sleep."*

<u>The prayer</u>:

Lord Jesus, who dost love me,
O spread Thy wings above me,
    And shield me from alarm!
Though Satan would devour me,
Let angels guards sing o'er me:
This child of God shall meet no harm.

My loved ones, rest securely,
For God this night will surely
    From perils guard your heads;
Sweet slumbers may He send you,
And bid His hosts attend you,
And through the night watch o'er your beds.

From: Now Rest Beneath Night's Shadows # 551, St. 4,5 <u>Lutheran Hymnary</u>
3/16/79
With all my love, Dad

How do I end such a story? I don't end it – it will go right on – whether in print or in my thoughts and prayers. I am so thankful for the family that we have, how the Lord has taken care of us, and how He has given us all that we have needed for this life.

"How great is the love the Father has lavished on us, that we should be called children of God! And that is what we are!" I John 3:1

With all my love,
Mom and
Grandmother

≈

~ Appendices ~

≈

≈ **Christmas Letters**
≈ **Melvina Memories**
≈ **Article by Stephen Sielaff**
≈ **Lists of Important Dates**

I have copies of my Christmas letters from the years 1997 – 2010 which I decided to add here since they contain a lot of information from those years. Perhaps down the road they will be kind of fun to read again.

I am also including some interesting quotes from letters I received from ELS pastors and others at the time I was being honored for 25 years of service. The secretary, Mary Jane Tweit, sent out a notice encouraging others to send a message to me. I heard from quite a few of them, too many to quote all of them here. As you will notice some of them were wishing me well on my retirement, but I didn't retire. I am still here ☺, not full-time but part-time, and now working in the Archives.

Christmas 1995

Dear Family and Friends,

Holiday greetings to you all!

This morning, December 8th, I woke up to a real blast of winter. Our neighbor was snowblowing our driveway which had about a foot of snow in it. Almost unbelievable since yesterday there was no snow on the ground Marie was ecstatic because school was called off — teacher and pupils love a "snow day." She started taking up golf a year ago and is fast becoming addicted to it. She is also excited about being drafted for jury duty during January and February. • • • Joel graduated from law school at the University of North Dakota in May, and following a summer of intensive studying for the bar exam he received news in October that he had "passed the bar." We are so thankful for such good news.. He is working for a law firm in Pine River, Minnesota. Since he's quite an outdoorsman he enjoys the fishing, hunting and cross country skiing up there in the lake country. • • • Jonathan is continuing to work on his PhD in economics at Berkeley, CA. He keeps very busy with studies and will be able to concentrate more fully on writing his thesis now that he is finishing his course work.• • • Sarah and Ron manage a pretty busy household — Jennie, Shawna, and Abby keep things humming with school and all the other activities they are involved in, Sarah has piano pupils, Ron has his teaching duties and together they provide all the good things they need to do for their lovely family. • • • Ted lives in Boston, near the Harvard campus. Research is his specialty and that takes him into many interesting fields. We thought it was neat that he was part of a research team doing some work for Disney this year. • • • I had reason to celebrate with a "Mortgage Burning Party" in August since I made my last house payment that month. To mark the end of fifteen years of house payments I had a Scandinavian cupboard built for my kitchen. A good friend from Norseland, Rachel Anthony, designed it for me and another good friend, a former seminary student and now pastor, James Krueger, built it. With their combined talents it turned out to be a beautiful addition to my kitchen. • • • I didn't take any big trips this year but am looking forward to going to California late in June for a grandniece's wedding. I still have my job working as secretary to the seminary and synod presidents and love it very much.

I wish you all a very joyous and blessed Christmas!

Melvina

Appendices

Christmas 1996

Dear Family and Friends,

I am sitting here in my office at the newly-constructed seminary and synod building into which we recently moved. I can't begin to tell you what a beautiful building it is and what a privilege it is for me to continue working as secretary to the synod and seminary presidents. There is a spectacular view from my office window which overlooks the city of Mankato. The Christmas card picture is taken in my new working area which is very comfortable and provides a pleasant working environment. I share this office with another secretary, Mary Jane Tweit, who works every afternoon. It has been very helpful to have a co-worker and it gives me a chance to get home a little earlier in the afternoons and makes it a lot easier to take a day off occasionally....This past summer I took a trip to Californhia for my grandniece Holly's, wedding. Sarah and Marie also came out and we had a wonderful time visiting Jonathan and all the other relatives there. We did a lot of sightseeing around San Francisco, rode the ferry, visited a winery, (the best part is all the tasting), walked through Golden Gate Park (one of Jonathan's favorite places), visited the Monterey Aquarium and did lots of shopping with my nieces, Chris and Nancy, who must be some of the world's best shoppers. Oh yes, we also went to a flea market which is a must if you are out there. I did pretty well keeping up with everyone on all these treks even though I turned 7o this summer. Marie had a nice party for me at the Country Pub.... We look forward to having Ted home for Christmas He has a new job at Harvard University doing research for the Office of Development....Ron, Sarah, Jennie, Shawna, and Abby will be here — traveling on Christmas Day since their program is on Christmas Eve. I haven't seen my granddaughters for 7 months and am very anxious for them to come. Jonathan will not be able to come but plans to make a trip back in the spring. Compared to living in California, this Minnesota winter would be quite a jolt. This year he has taken some courses in music composition and music appreciation, something he enjoys very much.... Joel, the attorney in the family, is working for a law firm in Pine River, Minnesota. He lives in Walker and works there two days a week for the same law firm. Marie and I have visited him several times and enjoy going up to the Lake Country. There is a wonderful Scandinavian store in Walker called "Liten Hus" where I can shop while Marie and Joel are out golfing....Marie keeps her classroom humming at Mt. Olive. She has twenty-one pupils in the 5th and 6th grades. She is a big help to me — even lets me drive her Explorer to work when the roads are bad. ... My brother Orlando passed away in November. It was hsad to lose my last brother, but I hope to see him again some day. At one of our Advent services we sang a hymn with this verse and I thought it would make an appropriate closing for my letter.

> Let my near and dear ones be
> Always near and dear to Thee.
> O bring me and all I love
> To Thy happy home above.

~ Melvina L. Aaberg ~

Christmas 1997

Dear Family and Friends,

Merry Christmas to all of you! It is such a wonderful time of the year when we again celebrate our Savior's birth.

I want to tell you a little bit about the trip Marie and I took to Norway this past summer. Norway is just the most beautiful country, the people are so friendly, the food is so good, it is so clean, and the scenery is spectacular! We spent a couple of days by ourselves, took a tour for seven days which went from Oslo to Bergen and back again, and spent a week in Lillehammer where our dear friend Berit (some of you have met her) was our gracious host. She took us to Kvam to visit the site where my Grandmother Olina and my Great Grandfather came from and up into the higher mountains to see the glaciers, the huge waterfalls which come roaring down the mountain and many other interesting places, museums, etc. We did lots of shopping in Norway, especially Lillehammer. I justified my shopping spree by telling myself it was my one and only trip over there, but now I am not so sure. We would both love to go back. My picture this year was taken at a park close to the Oslo harbor.

My family is fine— Ted is coming next Saturday for a week - he's going to help me make lefse. Sarah and family drive here on Christmas Day since Jennie, Shawna, and Abby are in the Christmas Eve program at their church. Jennie will be confirmed in May. Marie is very busy teaching at Mt. Olive and is right now baking cookies in the kitchen. Jonathan will not be home but I hope to go out to California next summer and visit him and also my two nieces and their families. Joel moved from up north to the cities last spring. He is doing some independent contract work for Medtronics and also works part-time for a law firm in Stillwater. It is nice to have him closer by.

I continue to enjoy my work very much and it is so nice to have another secretary, Mary Jane Tweit, with whom to share the work.

One more thing — I got a new car — a Saturn. It is champagne in color, has a moon roof, a spoiler, and power locks with keyless entry. Pretty snazzy!

With love and best wishes for a Merry Christmas and Happy New Year.

Melvina

Christmas 1998

Dear Family and Friends,

Have you ever heard of the village of Melvina? Many times I have driven past the big green sign on I-90 near Sparta, Wisconsin, which reads "MELVINA" but never took the time to take the exit. Rev. James Olsen, whom I have known since 1947 when I was his teacher at Norseland Christian Day School, and who lives near that little village, encouraged me to come and visit "my town." Marie and I did just that one Saturday in early November. It was a gorgeous, sunny day as we drove into Melvina which is nestled amongst the hills of the beautiful Melvina Valley. We made the acquaintance of a very nice lady there who invited us into her home and gave us some information on the history of that little village. I learned that a man by the name of Captain Hunt, who had served in the Wisconsin Cavalry during the Civil War, came to this place when the war was over and named it after his wife whose name was "Melvina." I have never met another person with my name though I have heard there are a few. There is also a street in Chicago and one in Milwaukee with that name, but I have been mostly impressed that there is an actual little village with my name, and, as I learned on this trip, there is also a Melvina Valley. Marie was busy with her camera that day and that's how this Christmas card came to be.

For my vacation this year I took a trip to California where I visited my son Jonathan and my nieces Nancy and Christine and their families. I always love going out there; we did a lot of sightseeing, visited a couple wineries, shopped (we never tire of that) and Jon made sure I got my first cable car ride this time. Marie and I get to West Bend a few times a year so we can keep up on Ron and Sarah and their active family. Jennie and Shawna are both great volleyball players and Abby is going to follow right along in her sisters' footsteps. I am proud of them all. Ted was able to spend some time here this summer and has been a big help getting me "more organized" in the garage and basement, by putting up some pegboard and shelves for me. It is quite an improvement. Maybe next year I will go out to Boston and spend a few days with him - another great place to visit.

Joel shot a couple of deer this year and he was so excited about it since it had been a few years since he had gotten any, a "drought", as he put it. He is now part owner of a small farm that he and a couple of friends are investing in. With its small lake and wooded area, it will prove to be a good spot for recreation and relaxation.

I am still enjoying my job very much. Many say our building has the best view in all of Mankato and I believe it is true.

I want to wish you all a very happy and blessed Christmas and will close with the same prayer I used a couple of years ago.

Let my near and dear ones be
Always near and dear to Thee.
O bring me and all I love
To Thy happy home above.

~ Melvina L. Aaberg ~

Christmas 1999

Dear Family and Friends,

The Aabergs are so happy to be receiving a new member into the family. As you can see by the picture, my son Joel has found a helpmate, a wonderful girl Deanna. She is so special to us and we adore her. We thank God for this wonderful blessing.

Christmas Eve will be spent at my home with Ted, Marie, Joel, Deanna, and myself in the traditional Norwegian style of reading the Christmas Gospel, singing Christmas Carols, and opening our gifts.

Sarah, Ron, Jennie, Shawna, and Abby will be coming over from Wisconsin to join us on Christmas Day. Their arrival is always a highlight. Jonathan won't be with us for Christmas and we will miss him, but we hope to see him in April when he makes a trip home.

Last summer my niece Nancy and her two children, Michael and Sarah, came for a visit. We had such fun showing them around the Duluth and North Shore area with Joel as our tour guide, the North Shore being one of his favorite spots. Ted also joined us back in Mankato and we were able to make a one-day trip to Tracy to visit relatives.

I took a short trip to Boston in November to visit son Ted and also joined up with my niece Christine and her husband Bill who was out there on a business trip. We had great fun and this time Ted was our tour guide.

Marie is in the kitchen baking cookies - a nice change from her teaching duties at Mt. Olive. I must say she is very good at both jobs. And I can't begin to tell you how much she does for me at home. I appreciate her so much.

My home has taken on a new look especially in the living room and dining room areas. I am so happy with this "new look" and I attribute this to my dear friend, Rachel Anthony, from Norseland. We spent an afternoon together at Sherwin Williams and things began to happen. We picked out wallpaper, border, paint ... a few days later carpeting and linoleum ... and still later we got pictures hung. She has helped me so often in so many ways.

I continue to work as secretary at the Seminary/Synod office in Mankato, a job I love very much. I enjoy the various aspects of my work as well as the people with whom I work. It keeps me in touch with the Synod and also with the seminary students who always brighten my day.

> *We gather round Thee, Jesus dear,*
> *So happy in Thy presence here;*
> *Grant us, our Savior, every one,*
> *To stand in heaven before Thy throne.*
> *Lutheran Hymnary 179, v. 6*

I wish you all a very joyous and blessed Christmas,

Melvina

Christmas 2000

Dear Family and Friends,

This past weekend Marie and I enjoyed a wonderful visit with Joel and Deanna in the cities. We did some fun things -- made lefse Saturday morning, shopped a little in the afternoon, and were treated to a performance of Dickens "Christmas Carol" at the Guthrie Theater in the evening. Deanna had gotten tickets 3rd row from the front through Medtronics where she works. Joel had broken his ankle a few days before so he was getting used to hobbling around on crutches. He works at EMPI which is a company that makes medical equipment.

This summer my only trip was to St. Mary's Hospital in Rochester where I had surgery to repair a hole between the atrium chambers of my heart. Marie provided excellent care for me during my recuperation. It really put a dent in her golfing and knowing how much she loves golfing it was quite a sacrifice. I appreciated it very much as well as the care and concern of all of my children and friends.

Marie got a real thrill in her teaching career this fall when her class won a state-wide competition in Minnesota sponsored by Best Buy, Target, the Tribune, and the Vikings. The project consisted of lesson plans each week called "Gridiron Geography" and the production of a 12' long US map showing what they had learned. They won a trip to Winter Park and were treated "royally." There were 650 teachers and 18,000 pupils who participated so it was really very special.

Jonathan came home in June to join with family and friends in celebrating Joel and Deanna's wedding reception. It was the first time in a long while we had the family all together and for such a joyous occasion, I count it as a real blessing. While Jon was home Ted, Jon, and I took a "roots" trip to areas around Tracy and Garvin where I grew up. It was very interesting and brought back a lot of memories. Ted's specialty is research so I know he is going to look more into family history while he is home now at Christmas.

The Mehlberg family continues to keep up a busy pace. Ron with his teaching, coaching track, and lots of transporting the girls to and fro; Sarah busy cooking good meals for her family, giving lots of piano lessons; and the girls with their school work and games. Jennifer and Shawna did very well on the volleyball team this year. Kettle Moraine took first place in the Conference. They have both joined Volleyball Clubs to keep them in shape this winter. Abby is a 5th grader and does very well in school but does love a day off now and then so she can curl up in the reclining chair and watch TV. She kept pretty close tabs on the election this year too -- pretty interested for a girl her age.

It still feels great to come to work at the seminary and synod office building every weekday morning. There is nothing I would rather do.

I will close with the first verse of one of my favorite Christmas hymns.

> Thy little ones, dear Lord, are we,
> And come Thy lowly bed to see;
> Enlighten ev-'ry soul and mind,
> That we the way to Thee may find.

Melvina

Christmas 2001

Dear Family and Friends,

This has been a year of celebrations. I completed 25 years as secretary at the ELS Seminary and the office. It all began back in 1976 when my husband, Ted, became President of Bethany Lutheran Th Seminary. I am still active in this position which keeps me in touch with many wonderful people. I am privileged served in this way for so many years.

This past summer was another celebration. All of my family celebrate my 75th birthday. The coming together of their special talents resul grand 3-day celebration which started out at Joel and Deanna's hom Louis Park on a Friday and ended up at my home in Mankato on Sunde beautiful weather made it possible to enjoy many festivities outdoors. I am thankful to my family for making my 75th birthday so sp was treated like a "queen."

In October we celebrated with the Mehlberg family in Wisc Jennie and Shawna, who both played as middle blockers for the Moraine Girls' Volleyball Team, had the excitement of going to the tournament this year where their team took 2nd place in Division 3. They are both tall and slender and very players. Their coach made the comment that "they can jump and they can jump all day." Abby is not far behi sisters in her accomplishments. Volleyball is her favorite too but she also plays basketball, and softball in the summer

The grandest celebration of all happened on October 10, 2001, when my lovely 4th granddaughter, Nicole Aaberg came into this world. She is the daughter of Joel and Deann and is so precious and loved. joy she has brought to the whole Aaberg family! I can't express how thankful we are for this wonderful gift. S baptized on December 22, 2001, at Norseland Lutheran Church where her grandfather had been pastor. It memorable day! She and her mother and father are now residing in a beautiful new home in East Bethel which makes you feel as though you are getting up north in the woods.

I wish you all a very joyous and blessed Christmas.

Love,
Melvina

Appendices

Christmas 2002

Dear Family and Friends,

Merry Christmas to all of you! As we celebrate this joyous season of Christmas may we always stay on the real meaning of Christmas, the birth of the Christ Child.

There were several events year. **Marie** was honored at a grand commemorating her 25 years in the taking a sabbatical and has been doing Rochester. Her favorite area of service always comes home with a smile so I in September and Marie and I took a packed many activities into a few days. enjoyed driving through New autumn colors. We also enjoyed Harvard Law School where Ted has his we can't go to Boston without doing a the Downtown Crossing and checked which we celebrated in our fami reception at Mt. Olive on M: classroom as a teacher. This year volunteer work at St. Mary's Hos; is that of a surgical messenger know she has enjoyed it. **Ted** tur trip to Boston to celebrate with hi Since we were there in Octob Hampshire and Rhode Island to vi touring the new Alumni Cen office. We were impressed. Of little shopping. We took the Bost out Macy's and Filene's.

Jennifer, my first granddaughter, graduated from Moraine Lutheran High School in June and was honored to be the salutatorian of her class. She is now pursui studies at MLC in New Ulm. **Shawna**, my second granddaughter, shared the excitement of the entire volleyball team as they took first place at the State Volleyball Tournament in Green Bay, WI. Then comes who is such a sweetheart – she pays a lot of attention to detail, is always prepared and ready for church on tir looks like a fashion plate when she steps out of her room. Now for **Clair**, the little daughter of Joel and D She is a little over 14 months old and we marvel at all that she is learning. Her parents read to her a lot and s learned to enjoy the books for listening rather than chewing on the corners. She is a beautiful girl, good n; and smart. Joel is teaching her to play ball, and hopefully she will learn to love fishing. If she follows mother's footsteps she will also be a great cook and homemaker..

We enjoyed **Jonathan's** visit last summer. He happened to be here on my birthday and baked m; He's great at making lefse and kringla among other things. He has so many talents in addition to his writi; music. **Sarah** teaches piano lessons several days a week at KML and takes an active role in the musical conc the West Bend community. **Ron** is a valuable teacher on the staff at KML – teaching religion and Latin. He busy providing for his family and all that that entails.

As for me – even though I had thought of retiring this fall, I am continuing to work – now for the elected Synod President, John A. Moldstad. He encouraged me and gave me such a good pep talk to co working, and Seminary President, Gaylin Schmeling, gave me a raise. Needless to say, I enjoy my work very m

May you all have a blessed Christmas and Happy New Year.

~ Melvina L. Aaberg ~

Christmas 2003

Dear Family and Friends,

This noon I had the pleasure of going over to Marie's classroom at Mt. Olive where her 5ᵗʰ and 6ᵗʰ graders present[ed] of Christmas Carols on their recorders. They did very well for such young musicians. Marie was featured in the issue of MAYO TODAY magazine with a two-page article about the volunteer work she had done there during he[r] she even making the cover. A summary of the article also appeared in the *Lutheran Sentinel*.

In October I flew to Boston to visit Ted. He's a great host. We traveled to 3 other states – not hard to do from B[o] Hampshire, Rhode Island, and Maine. A special highlight was walking the *Marginal Way*, a path along the Atlanti[c] Ogunquit, Maine. Ted has lots of hobbies – the most recent is playing the piano. He purchased a Roland Keybo[ard] and has been practicing diligently. He'll be home for Christmas.

Sarah has gone back to teaching this year. Whereas she used to be busy giving piano lessons she now is busy corre[cting] and teaching 4ᵗʰ graders at Good Shepherd Lutheran School. Abby is in 8ᵗʰ grade and Jennie and Shawna are both Martin Luther College in New Ulm. That leaves Ron driving alone to Kettle Moraine for the first time in 5 year[s]. Next year Abby will accompany him when she joins the high school crowd. Jennie and Shawna were both in the and are in the treble choir. Jennie was thrilled to make the dance team which performs at home basketball games. them during the holidays.

Jonathan, a man of many talents, has written a children's book The *Laplander Goose*. In addition to that he has [made] several CD's. One that really brought back memories was from a tape made when I visited brother Marvin several y[ears] CA. We were taking turns peddling away on the player piano he had at that time and Marvin, the entertainer that he put himself into it. Many of our relatives have enjoyed that CD. Jonathan was home for a visit last summer and ju[st] help pick out a new computer for me. The timing was perfect.

Joel, Deanna, and Clair will be here for Christmas. We got together and made lefse before Thanksgiving. The mak[ing] is not going to be a lost art in my family because every one of my children can make it. It has been such a blessing t[o] granddaughter Clair within easy driving distance from us. Marie and I love taking care of her and can't wait for [her to] and stay overnight at Gramma's and Auntie Re's so Mommy and Daddy can take a vacation. The enclosed pictur[e] Thanksgiving Day.

I am still working at the seminary and synod offices. Every once in awhile I hear how older people are go[ing] work—with me I just never quit. I love it too much.

May God grant each of you a blessed Christmas and a Happy New Year.

> We gather round Thee, Jesus dear,
> So happy in Thy presence here;
> Grant us, our Savior, ev'ry one,
> To stand in heav'n before Thy throne.

Melvina

Appendices

2004

Dear Family and Friends:

Here it is December 20th and even though I retired from my full-time job at the end of August I am just getting around to starting my yearly Christmas letter. In answer to many people's questions, "Are you enjoying your retirement?" Yes, I am, but I also look forward to working about 3 half-days a week, partly in the ELS Archives and partly in the Museum where I am back doing a little work for former ELS Pres. George Orvick. It keeps me in touch with many wonderful friendships that have so enriched my life over the past 28 years. I had some great retirement parties and am grateful to everyone who had a part in making those so special for me. I can say, " I now have the best of both worlds."

Today I am up at Joel's in East Bethel – icy roads prevented me from returning home as planned. As I look out the window I see huge piles of split wood where people in this small neighborhood have stocked up their supply for the winter. Joel, Deanna and Clair now enjoy a fireplace in the lower level of their home – pretty cozy. Yesterday we all made lefse, (including Clair) who is fast becoming a baker – thanks to her mother's patience in training her. I found out she can even crack eggs by herself. Clair (3) loves playing house – I am the baby and she is the mommy.

Marie ventured out on a new career after 26 years of teaching school. She is now employed by the Mayo Clinic in Rochester as Coordinator of the Young Adult Volunteers. She is learning a lot, is very busy and loves it very much – I know they are well pleased with her work there. Even though she has an apartment in Rochester, she is home most weekends and continues to help me in many ways.

It has been so nice to have Ted home in July and again for a week in November, plus now at Christmas. The highlight of the November visit was to take in a piano recital at MacPhail's School of Music in Minneapolis given by his best buddy from Scarville days, Dan Sabo. Teddy and Danny were together almost from day one until high school when they went their separate ways. They made a great pair playing baseball (two teams – Dan's team and Ted's team) they made it work somehow in that little town of 70 people –pretty creative little boys. Dan's recital was an outstanding performance and we were so proud. Lots of good things came out of Scarville, Iowa.

Sarah continues to teach 4th grade at Good Shepherd in West Bend, WI. Abby is now a freshman at Kettle Moraine Luth. High School where she takes, among other classes, Latin from her father, as did her sisters before her. Jennie and Shawna are both studying to be teachers at Martin Luther College in New Ulm. I know they are both working very hard and enjoying school. Sarah is especially pleased with the way they are coming along with their piano lessons. She may get some pianists out of her daughters yet.

Thanks to Ted and Jonathan my extra bedroom has been turned into a very comfortable (office/computer room). Now I have no excuse for not working on my "Journal" which the children are all anxious for me to do. First Ted came home and in about three days time we had moved everything out, painted the walls, and had the carpet installed. A couple of weeks later Jon came and the very next morning we made a trip to the IKEA store where we purchased a computer desk, bookshelf and another small chest for the scanner. That evening Jon assembled them, and in the next few days did all kinds of good things to my computer which really make it fun for me to work on. I am keeping pace with the 21st Century. I call it a Scandinavian room because we decorated it by using a lot of my Norwegian artifacts - including hardanger curtains. It is partly Swedish, of course, because of the Swedish IKEA store, but that is OK

I close with a verse from one of my favorite Christmas hymns and wish you all a very joyous and blessed Christmas!

> *We gather round Thee, Jesus dear,*
> *So happy in Thy presence here;*
> *Grant us, our Savior, every one,*
> *To stand in heaven before Thy throne.*
> *ELH 144 v. 8*

Melvina

~ Melvina L. Aaberg ~

> On Jordan's bank the heralds cry
> Announces that the Lord is nigh;
> Awake and hearken, for he brings
> Glad tidings of the King of kings.

Dear Family and Friends,

It always takes awhile to get started on my Christmas letter but I just had a phone call from daughter Sarah who is always so peppy and it rubbed off on me so I am going to begin. Every year there are many fun and important things to write about and 2005 is no exception. In June Sarah and I flew to Boston to visit Ted. Boston is so full of interesting places to visit and sites to see but the highlight of this trip was when Ted took us to hear the Boston Pops as they presented their patriotic Flag Day concert in Symphony Hall. That was such a treat!

Joel turned 40 in August and Deanna surprised him with a big party. On a beautiful Saturday afternoon people began to arrive -- some with RVs, some with tents for camping out overnight -- friends from school days, neighbors, coworkers, and family A video had been made compiling special events in Joel's life from day one and on which was played many times throughout the day as new guests arrived.. Jon had a lot to do with that project. It was a very special time.

August was the month for birthdays -- I turned 79 this year. We celebrated out on my patio which Joel and Deanna had put in for me last summer and which was extended this summer by putting in an area for bedding plants. Clair finished the job when she got the hose and did the watering. It was a special treat to have niece Christine and husband Bill here from San Jose, also Ron, Sarah, Jennie, Shawna and Abby from West Bend. Marie, with her ever-ready camera, took a picture of me with my 4 lovely granddaughters -- something I have wanted for a long time. Picture is enclosed.

By October I was on my way to CA to attend niece Nancy's wedding. It was a grand celebration in her own back yard. The theme was Hawaiian which meant even the guests were wearing Hawaiian attire. CA is always a favorite place to go. It was wonderful to keep in touch with the nieces and nephews out there and, of course, shopping with the girls -- no wine tasting this time. Several days were spent in San Francisco with Jonathan. What a great city to visit. I found that public transportation is not too hard to figure out in SF. One of the highlights of that trip was a 2 1/2 hour long walking tour of the Victorian Houses. I learned that when 3 colors are used in painting the exterior of the house it qualifies as a Painted Lady. Another highlight was a stroll through the Golden Gate Park and especially the Japanese Gardens. There are so many small restaurants right off the street where you can watch through the window as they prepare their delicacies -- the crepes were my favorite.

Marie comes home nearly every weekend and is always filled with wonderful stories about her work at the Mayo Clinic as coordinator of the young adult volunteers. One weekend she painted two walls in my kitchen (Strawberry/Rhubarb). It took 3 coats and it really gave my kitchen a lift and put new life into me as well.

Now for a little bit about Clair who turned 4 on October 10th. I am so blessed to have a granddaughter who is within about 2 hours driving distance from here. She loves to bake kringla and I can't believe how those little fingers are learning to make the pretzel twists. She can measure flour, crack the eggs and do most anything. Now she is in gymnastics so there's always something new to learn.

I am still working part-time in the Archives and Museum -- it helps to keep me in the mix of things and I love my work there so much.

I wish you all a Merry Christmas and a happy, healthy New Year.

Melvina

༄༅༄༅༄༅༄༅༄༅༄༅༄༅༄༅༄༅༄༅༄༅༄༅༄༅༄༅༄༅༄༅༄༅༄༅༄༅

Christmas 2006

Dear Family and Friends,

The year 2006 has been a memorable one – I turned 80 in August and lots of good things happened in celebration of that event. On Memorial Day weekend Ted and Joel upgraded my kitchen with a new stainless steel sink and counter tops. It turned out perfect and I enjoy it very much. In July, Marie took me on a two-week trip to Norway where we were privileged to stay at the home of Tor Jakob Welde, his wife Reiko, and daughter Miriam. Tor, a former Bethany Seminary student is now pastor in his homeland of Norway. A highlight of our trip was hearing him preach in his home congregation at Avaldsnes. We are grateful for the many kindnesses we enjoyed as guests in their home – the lovely meals prepared by Reiko, the violin performances by Miriam and the evening devotions by Tor. Miriam is a promising young violinist who at the age of nine years performed as guest violinist with the Bergen Philharmonic Orchestra for their 2006 New Year's concert. The reviews in the Bergen paper reported "that would have been quite a feat for an adult but for a nine year old it was sensational." One of the reasons for our trip to Norway was to look up the "Aaberg Roots." Without the help of Tor this never would have been accomplished. He took us on a two-day trip through more than 46 tunnels and beautiful mountain scenery to Sogndal, the place from which the Aabergs had emigrated. Through contact with Olav Johannas Åberge (doesn't mean we were related) who lived on a narrow winding road called Aberge, we were shown exactly where the Aabergs had lived. That trip is a wonderful story in itself, but too much for my Christmas letter.

Getting on toward August – invitations started coming for my 80th birthday party to be held on August 5th at Joel, Deanna, and Clair's spacious home in East Bethel. The face on the invitation had the caption *"Auntie Melvina"* and looked like me but the body was definitely more glamorous – it was that of *Auntie Mame*, one of Warner Bros. Boardway Classics. Jonathan was in charge of invitations. Ted picked up the title and used it on the cover of *"Auntie Melvina's Top Ten Recipes"* which he published in commemoration of the event, and which has already gone through a second printing. Jonathan put together a DVD "story of my life" which had its first official showing at the party. It was so well done and real – at times bringing tears to my eyes, and to others. Only Jonathan could come up with something like that. It will be my treasure. Now a little bit about Sarah and Ron along with their three lovely daughters: Jennie, 5th year MLC; Shawna, 4th year MLC; and Abby 3rd year, KML. Sarah had been busy at home baking and preparing lots of good things for the weekend. To make it complete niece Nancy and daughter Sarah flew in from CA – it was such fun having them there. On Sunday morning we all gathered around while Ron led us in a brief devotion and Ted closed with a prayer after which we all sang *"Now Thank We All Our God."* We all enjoyed being together at Joel and Deana's lovely *"home in the woods"* for the better part of three days and nights. It was truly a Birthday Bonanza!

Merry Christmas and may God bless you all as we again celebrate our Savior's birth.

Melvina

Christmas 2007
On Jordan's bank the heralds cry
Announces that the Lord is nigh;
Awake and hearken, for he brings
Glad tidings of the King of kings.

Dear Family and Friends,

The hymn verse quoted above was used in my Christmas letter a couple of years ago, but I decided to print it again. Our dear Norwegian friend, Tor Jakob Welde, remarked how he loved this hymn and it is one which they do not have in their Norwegian hymnary. So, Tor, this is for you.

It always takes awhile to get down to the business of writing my Christmas letter. I like to think about special things that are important to me and that others might like to read. We didn't have any big family celebrations this year but any get-togethers with my family are always dear to my heart. Last summer Jonathan came for a long weekend to visit and that was a special time. He's talented in so many areas and there are always a lot of good things to talk about. He and I enjoyed watching *Sweet Land*, a wonderful love story about Norwegian settlers in this country years ago. Jon is great at helping me with my computer questions—even long distance by phone he has helped me out of a jam many times. Marie and I flew to Boston in October to visit Ted. He's a great host, a very good cook, and continues to enjoy his work at Harvard. We traveled to five New England states—Marie is keeping track of all she has visited so far—not many left to go. The weather was perfect and the trees were ablaze with color, especially around Lexington and Concord. In Ogunquit, Maine, we hiked *Marginal Way* trail which weaves along the rugged coastline of the Atlantic Ocean. Marie is a good traveling companion. She is also very good at her job at Mayo Clinic where she is coordinator of the Young Adult Volunteers. Her program has really grown in the 3 1/2 years she has been there. She comes home nearly every weekend and helps me with many chores around the house and yard. We like going to Dunn Brothers for coffee.

My first granddaughter, Jennifer Mehlberg, graduated from MLC last May with a degree in Early Childhood and Elementary Education. She is now director and teacher of the Early Childhood Center at Crown of Life Lutheran Church in Ft. Myers, FL. It is quite an undertaking to begin a new school but it is going well under her capable leadership. Next May, Shawna, granddaughter #2, graduates with the same degree and it will be exciting to see where she begins her career. This first semester she served as an assistant teacher for one of her professors. That says something about her ability, doesn't it? Then Abby, granddaughter #3, graduates from Kettle Moraine Lutheran High School next spring. Her future plans for college I have yet to find out. She's quite a girl and has a lot of good ideas about many things. Sarah is busy teaching 4th grade at Good Shepherd Lutheran School and I know whoever gets her for a teacher is blessed. The same goes for her husband Ron who teaches religion and Latin at Kettle Moraine. He is also very highly thought of in his profession there.

I have been so blessed to have Joel, Deanna, and Clair living within pretty easy driving distance from Mankato. This makes it possible to spend quite a bit of time with Clair, granddaughter #4. Big thing for her this year was starting kindergarten. Since her parents have read to her from early on she is quite a reader already and was promoted to the enriched reading class. She also is developing many homemaking skills. She's made Kringla since she was three, and this year she took over rolling Lefse (using the big rolling pin) and it amazed us all how she could handle that. Joel and Deanna have put a lot of work into finishing their basement this year. It is so cozy down there with a beautiful fireplace, bookshelves, carpeting, and a corner bar with a special cooler for wine. Their home has gotten to be quite a gathering place for family and they can accommodate a lot of people. Most of our family will be enjoying New Year's festivities there. One more thing . . . they got a puppy last summer, a German short hair – his name is Buddy and he's growing up fast. When he gets older Joel hopes he will be a hunting dog as well as a good friend for Clair.

I continue to work in the archives M/W/F mornings and some hours in the museum during afternoons. However, since George Orvick's book *Forget Not All His Benefits* has come off the press, I do not have as much work to do over there right now. For the past couple of months the archivist, Paul Madson, and I have been working on getting all of my husband Ted's important papers, correspondence, some of his sermons, Bible study topics, seminary class notes, and many other things too numerous to mention ready for storage. This is very important work to ensure their preservation for future generations. Ted and Paul were good friends and it has been nice working with him on this project as we come across many things that bring back a lot of memories.

Melvina

Christmas 2008

Thy little ones, dear Lord, are we,
And come Thy lowly bed to see;
Enlighten every soul and mind,
That we the way to Thee may find.

Dear Family and Friends,

The other day I was thinking about Christmas when I was a young child in Sunday School and our class was practicing this hymn for the children's program. I attended church and Sunday School at a little chapel located in Garvin, Minnesota. A short distance out of town is where I lived with my Aunt Marie and Uncle Olaf. The little chapel is still there but no longer used for worship services. Years later it is nice to have those memories.

This is the first time that Jonathan has been home for Christmas for several years and that makes it so special for our family. He and Ted came early - Jon from San Francisco and Ted from Boston. They are doing many things for me – preparing tasty meals, baking cookies, shopping, etc. One afternoon we enjoyed an enchanting production of the Nutcracker presented by the Mankato Ballet Company. It was held in St. Peter and because of the weather no travel was advised, but we went anyway, and thankfully made it safely.

Marie is going on her 5th year as Coordinator of the Young Adult Volunteers at Mayo Clinic. For the past several months she has also filled in as Coordinator of the Mayo Clinic Volunteer Services. Hopefully that position will soon be filled. She comes home most weekends and does a lot of chores for me. She's great at making sure my supply of groceries is adequate. We love playing Chinese Checkers and sometimes take our board to play at Dunn Bros Coffee.

Ron and Sarah are now "empty nesters." Jennie and Shawna both teach in Florida. "Early Childhood" is their specialty. Jennie is in her 2nd year at Crown of Life in Ft. Myers and Shawna is at Divine Savior Academy in Doral, a suburb of Miami. They are only 2+ hours apart. How neat is that! Abby started college at MLC this fall. It appears she is going to follow in her sisters' footsteps. Sarah continues to teach 4th grade at Good Shepherd and Ron at Kettle Moraine Lutheran High School. I am very proud of them all. They are a family of teachers!

Joel, Deanna, and Clair (now 7) are a busy family. Joel and Deanna continue to work at Medtronic in St. Paul and Clair is a first grader at Cedar Creek School. We are proud of her reading, math and computer skills already at this young age. Since she lives the closest of my granddaughters I get to see her more often and that makes me happy. I am able to make the drive to their home in East Bethel by myself. Oh yes, not to forget Buddy, their dog. Joel had Buddy out hunting this year and he had a collision with a porcupine. Not too pleasant!

I continue to be blessed with good health. They say working keeps you young and maybe it does. I still work a few hours now and then at the Ottesen Museum, but more regularly Monday, Wednesday, Friday mornings at the ELS Archives. That work is so interesting, especially since many of the documents, correspondence, etc. that come up bring back a lot of memories.

We will have an all-family Christmas celebration at Joel and Deanna's between Christmas and New Years. Their home is the perfect place –beautifully surrounded by a wooded area. The lower level is so cozy, complete with fireplace, and lots of space for blow-up mattresses.

A very Merry and Blessed Christmas to all of you as we celebrate the birthday of our Lord and Savior Jesus Christ.

Melvina

~ Melvina L. Aaberg ~

Christmas 2009

Dear Family and Friends,

It's a sunny day today and a good time to work on my Christmas letter. I am listening to some wonderful Christmas music which always puts me in great spirits.

Ted will be coming on the 17th just in time to be my escort for the Bethany Christmas Banquet. He is doing very well. Even though he was laid off from Harvard during the economic crunch he is already working a couple of days a week at Boston University. With the skills he has there are several opportunities. He has become quite a craftsman too. He made Sarah a beautiful Nantucket bench for her birthday and for Marie's birthday he made a beautiful Chinese Checker Board. When Clair saw that she said, "I don't see HOW he could make that." Neither do I.

Sarah and Ron are both busy with their teaching careers and keeping in touch with their daughters. Jennie and Shawna are both teaching in Florida and enjoy teaching the three and four year olds in the Early Childhood Programs of their respective congregations. What a blessing for parents to have their little ones in the care of fine Christian teachers. Abby is in her 2nd year at Martin Luther College and is following in her sisters' footsteps. They are a family of teachers!

Marie is doing very well as Coordinator of the Young Adult Volunteers at the Mayo Clinic. Her program is growing steadily. She works with students from a variety of ethnic backgrounds. I have been around enough to know how much they love and respect her. She sold her Town Home and bought a home in a neighborhood. She really lucked out with some exceptionally fine neighbors.

Jonathan is so good at bringing holiday cheer to his neighborhood. One day he made 3 double batches of lefse and invited friends, neighbors and nearby shopkeepers to come by anytime for treats – and they did!. A few days later he made 1500 cookies which he delivered to many friends, coffee shops, businesses, etc. He said they do love lefse in San Franciso and also the children seem to prefer Kringla to cookies. I guess there's a little Norwegian in everybody.

Joel, Deanna and Clair live only a couple of hours away so Marie and I get up there quite frequently. Clair is 8 years old and in second grade. She's quite an entertainer, a very good reader, loves to play games, loves company and having sleepovers with her neighbor girl. She's also getting to know her way around the kitchen quite well for her age. Joel and Deanna are both working full time so it makes for a busy schedule. Joel was able to take his family with him to Switzerland this year when he traveled there on business. What a treat that was! I mustn't forget Buddy the dog, we love him too.

My nieces Nancy and Christine and husband Bill from California came in August to celebrate my 83rd birthday. Sarah also came from Wisconsin and Marie from Rochester. Those girls took over the kitchen and I had no work to do. Christine made a chocolate cheesecake, Sarah made a Scandinavian almond cake and Nancy made a delicious chicken breast dish. We had a feast together with some wine, of course. One day we also got in a quick trip to Tracy, but stopped in New Ulm on the way for some more very productive shopping.☺

Now about the picture: As you can see I had a bumper crop of apples this year. This came from a Minnesota Jonathan tree I had planted shortly after I purchased my home here. Thanks to my good neighbor Gary who used his 10 foot ladder to get the top ones down. I won't be buying apples for a long time.

May you all have a blessed Christmas as we celebrate the birth of the Christ Child.

Melvina

Appendices

Christmas 2010

Dear Family and Friends,

While 2009 was a big year for apples, 2010 was a big year for cherries. Thanks to my good neighbors, Gary and Sue, I am the one who has always benefited from their cherry tree - but no more, -it was losing branches and needed to be cut down. I also lost a wonderful apple tree this spring in a strong windstorm. Marie and I decided it made a good prop for picture taking. Joel will saw it into some great firewood.

Ted took me on a 10-day trip to California in July. He and Jonathan planned the itinerary and rented a car, which allowed us to enjoy many things including great parties at the homes of my nieces, Nancy and Christine together with their husbands, children, grandchildren and other family friends.

With Jon living in San Francisco we just needed to walk out on the sidewalk to realize what a close-knit neighborhood he lives in. We enjoyed visiting some of the quaint shops nearby. It isn't just the shops, it's the people who own and work in these shops that make them such fun to visit. We spent a day at Yosemite National Park and what a wonder to behold. Ted and Jon hiked all the way up the steep trail to the Bridal Veil Falls but I enjoyed it by sitting on a log halfway up. We traveled through gold mining country to visit good friends Phil and Barbara Lawrence in Nevada City, CA, and stayed at "Miners Inn" along the way - very appropriately named. Jon was an excellent host – his cozy apartment became our home, his cooking was superb, and his hospitality unbeatable.

. Now a little bit about my family. Even though Ted was laid off from his job at Harvard after the economic crunch hit, he has had part-time work nearly all the time. First working at Boston University then the Harvard Ed School and now back at the Harvard Law School on a part-time basis. This time he has the boss's office ☺. He's not the boss but he has his office. I think this is so neat.

I mentioned before that the Mehlberg family is a family of teachers and that is still very true. They are all teaching except for Abby who is hard at work in her third year at M LC. Jennie is now Coordinator for the entire WELS Southeast States Early Childhood Programs in addition to being director and teacher of her own school at Ft. Myers. Shawna does quite a bit of tutoring, coaching, etc., in addition to her regular teaching, plus she has become such a great cook (following in her mother's footsteps) that she is called upon to bring a dish to many potluck dinners.

Clair is nine years old - a good student and getting to be a good swimmer as well. I understand Joel is thinking about buying her a BB Gun. She gets to come along and pick out the color. Let's hope she takes to it so she can accompany her Dad on hunting trips later on. Joel and Deanna keep very busy with their jobs in addition to doing projects around their yard and home. We hope to gather there for our family party again this year between Christmas and New Years.

Marie comes home many weekends and is so good at seeing what needs to be done around my yard and house. She continues to enjoy her work as Coordinator of the Young Adult Volunteers at the Mayo Clinic. She loves owning her own home in Rochester and I enjoy getting to stay there whenever I come down for appointments or just to visit.

I continue to work in the Synod Archives every M/W/F mornings, a job which I enjoy very much. It keeps me in touch with the people I have worked with over the years as secretary at one time or another and that's an added bonus

A blessed Christmas to all of you as we celebrate the birthday of the Christ Child.

Welvina

Melvina Memories
Here are a couple of Melvina Memories:

"Back in the early 80s, when I was on the seminary faculty, there was one student who was consistently late for class. No amount of encouragement, extortion or threatening seemed to cure him of his tardiness habit. One day, in frustration, I went to Melvina and asked her if she had a key for the classroom door, and I explained to her that I thought the only way to cure this student of his bad habit would be to lock the classroom door at the beginning of the hour, so that he would have to knock and petition to be let in. I will always remember the eager cooperation I received from her, and the glee she expressed when she heard my plan, since she had become quite annoyed at this student's behavior as well. She supplied the key, and the next day the door was locked at the beginning of the hour. The student arrived late as usual, but was not admitted to the classroom that day. After that incident he was on time. ..."

Mark O. Harstad

". . . You were always so personable and yet professional. To be greeted by your sweet disposition, caring smile and conversation starters of genuine interest, you always made me feel welcomed. Thank you for faithful and diligently serving us in this capacity. You witnessed major changes in both institutions during your 28 years. Those transitions were accomplished in part to your pleasant and helpful way of adjusting and accommodating to the changes.
Your Kringla still remains my favorite cookie! . . ."
Glenn Obenberger

". . . When I was in seminary one of the inside "jokes" was that Melvina was actually running the synod, not Pres. Orvick. Over the years I have learned that this "joke" contains some measure of truth. Granted, Melvina does not have the authority sometimes ascribed to her, but where would our synod be without her? Her more than able assistance to Pres. Orvick and Pres. Moldstad, her gracious presence for anyone setting foot in the synod/seminary building, her amazing secretarial skills, her motherly manner to countless seminary students, her splendid example of being a Christian; all these traits and more make Melvina a truly special lady…"

Michael K. Smith

. . . It has always been a joy to see you, talk to you, and work with you. Your professionalism and personal nature were always wonderfully blended. We were so fortunate to have a woman of strong faith and talent to assist us in so many ways. May our Savior continue to bless you.

David Thompson

". . . In the all too short time I have had the privilege of getting to know you, and to be the recipient of kindnesses, too numerous to count, your always prompt responses to my e-mail, telephone or during Trustee meetings, requests were always deeply appreciated. Your many and varied contributions to the synod are legend and all of us will miss your being among us as we go about the work of His church.   You have been a blessing to the Evangelical Lutheran Synod as well as to each of us individually."

Wayne Anderson

". . . I am sure there were times when the work was overbearing. There also was the new technology with printers and the computers. Only once do I remember frustration setting in. There was one day, with an older photocopier, that I needed assistance because the machine had jammed and I couldn't fix the problem. You came to the back room, opened the side door of the machine and slammed it shut; opened the front cover and slammed it shut even harder. The machine lights came on and as you walked away you said, *'Sometimes you just have to be rough with it!'*

But as a seminary student, I only saw the smile of true concern. As a pastor I have only heard the voice of a friend. As a co-worker in the synod office, I have found someone who understands.

Thank you for these 28 years of friendship. May the Lord grant us many more years here and then an eternity together with Him!"

Craig Ferkenstad

Interview by Stephen Sielaff

Here I chose to insert a copy of the interview that Bethany College student, Stephen Sielaff, wrote about me. It was part of his class assignment for a class he took from Bethany professor, Dr. Ryan McPherson.

Stephen Sielaff
HIST460
Melvina Aaberg
5/7/10

"Theodore A. Aaberg 1925-1980." *Lutheran Sentinel,* 28 February 1980, 52-53.
Aaberg, Melvina. Interviewed by Stephen Sielaff, Mankato MN, 3 May 2010.

Melvina Aaberg was born Melvina Lorraine Olson on August 20, 1926, on a small farm around Garvin, Minnesota. She was the youngest of her family of five with four older brothers. Melvina was baptized on September 19, 1926, In Höland Lutheran Church, a member of the Norwegian Evangelical Lutheran Church. Both of her parents were of Norwegian descent. Her father, Edward Gabriel, passed away when she was only sixteen months old, and her mother, Jennie Amalia, died when she was only four years old. After her parents passed away her aunt and uncle, who lived nearby, became her legal guardians. Her four older brothers remained on the farm to maintain it. Despite the deaths of her parents and the depression that was ravaging the nation, she had a relatively normal childhood. Her favorite things to do as a child were to play with her dolls, and also go into the tool shed and tinker around with the tools.

She went to high school at Tracy High School. There she soon discovered that her favorite subjects were shorthand, accounting, typing and mathematics. Her enjoyment for these subjects would continue on into her college years when she attended Bethany Lutheran College. There she also developed a taste for music. It was then when she honed her piano and organ skills. Upon graduating she became a teacher at Norseland Christian Day School in St. Peter and later at Mount Olive Lutheran School in Mankato. It was during these years that she met her future husband, Theodore Arne Aaberg. She fondly remembers how he was too shy to talk to her when he saw her playing piano at a Christian day school meeting. She was delighted when he gained the courage to talk to her, and eventually court her. Theodore and she wed on October 8, 1951, at Zion Lutheran Church in Tracy, Minnesota.

Theodore Aaberg was a minister in the Evangelical Lutheran Synod and upon graduating from the seminary in 1949 was ordained that same year at Scarville Synod and Center Lutheran Churches in Iowa. He stayed at that parish for nineteen years. In 1968 he took a call to Norseland-Norwegian Grove parish. During these years when her husband was pastor, Melvina remained his closest friend and aid. She remembers baking for him and taking him cake on Saturday afternoons when he was working hard on the next day's sermon. In addition to being a phenomenal baker, she raised five wonderful children, three boys and two girls. She believes that her moist significant accomplishments in life include raising a family and being by her husband's side. In her spare time she practiced the art of Norwegian Rosemaling, which is decorative flower painting.

In 1976 Pastor Aaberg was called to be the first full-time president of Bethany Lutheran Theological Seminary. Melvina would become the secretary for the seminary, a position she would hold for 28 years. On January 8, 1980, four years after accepting the call, the Reverend Theodore Aaberg was taken from this world of suffering when he died of sarcoidosis. As seminary secretary, it was her responsibility to aid the president by overseeing the recordkeeping and the day-to-day operations. She was not only known for her secretarial skills, but also for her baking skills. Accordingly one of her other tasks which she undertook was baking goods like Norwegian kringla for the students and faculty. She currently serves in the Archives of the Evangelical Lutheran Synod. She enjoys working with the synod's historical records and making sense of them, while organizing the material for future generations.

When asked concerning her opinion on working at the seminary she said it was "wonderful, [and that she] can't say enough good about it." Over the years she has gotten to know generations of ministers. She commented on how she still receives Christmas cards and hugs at conferences. She has enjoyed getting to know each seminarian. She describes them as part of her "family." When she retired from her job as secretary, President Gaylin Schmeling planned a retirement party for her up at the Schwan's Retreat Center in Trego, Wisconsin. She had always wanted to go there but never had the opportunity. Many of her friends with whom she had worked over the years were there. She fondly remembers, "It was a beautiful place with great food and good company. I was treated like a 'queen'."

During her time at the seminary there were doctrinal debates ravaging the Lutheran synods. Issues concerning the doctrines of fellowship and the Lord's Supper and also issues concerning women's roles in the church were among those under contention. It was during these debates that Melvina was thankful she was only a secretary, and could go home and forget about them. However she never did leave her husband's side during these tough years. It was out of this that she developed her philosophy of life, which is to always live and keep your Christian faith.

Melvina came from a traditional Norwegian family. She enjoys eating lefse and kringla, but she does not like lutefisk. She neither likes the taste nor the texture. She currently is a member at Mount Olive Lutheran Church in Mankato, Minnesota.

Here I decided to put some dates that are handy to have for future reference and just to remember:

Parents

Theodore Arne Aaberg, born January 29, 1925. Wildrose, North Dakota.

Baptized February 22, 1925, by his father Rev. Theo. Aaberg.

Sponsors: Mr. & Mrs. C. E. Anderson, Hilmar Monger and Mr. C. Reebok.

Melvina Lorraine Olson, born August 20, 1926, in Lyon County Minnesota, at

Höland Norwegian Evangelical Lutheran Church, September 19, 1926.

Rev. U. L. Larsen, pastor, Sponsors: Mr. and Mrs. Olaf C. Olson,

Melvin Johnson and Emma Johnson.

Children:

Theodore Edward Aaberg, September 16, 1952, baptized at Naeve Hospital, Albert Lea, MN by his father, Pastor Theodore A. Aaberg, Affirmation of baptism on October 19, 1952, at Scarville Evangelical Lutheran Church, Scarville, IA. Honorary sponsors: Mrs. Alette Aaberg and Mr. Olaf C. Olson. Other sponsors were Rev. and Mrs. Paul Petersen, Miss Mildred Johnson and Mr. Joseph Aaberg. Theodore was confirmed on June 5th, 1966, at Center Lutheran Church rather than Scarville since he was in a class of four boys, three of them from that congregation: Jack Cox, David Storby, and Dale Olson. Lake Mils, IA.

Sarah Ann Aaberg, October 8, 1953, baptized at Naeve Hospital, Albert Lea, MN by her father, Pastor Theodore A. Aaberg. Affirmation of baptism on November 8, 1953, at Scarville Evangelical Lutheran Church, Scarville, IA. Sponsors: Mr. and Mrs. Carl Annexstad, Miss Hilma Dale and Mr. Clarence Dale. Sarah was confirmed on June 4, 1967 at Scarville Lutheran Church, Scarville IA.

Marie Elizabeth Aaberg, November 23, 1954, baptized at Naeve Hospital, Albert Lea, MN, by her father Pastor Theodore A. Aaberg. Affirmation of baptism on December 12, 1954, at Scarville Evangelical Lutheran Church, Scarville, IA. Sponsors: Mr. and Mrs. Arlin Zingg, Mr. Herman Aaberg, and Miss Ida Aaberg. Marie was confirmed on June 8, 1969, at Norseland Evangelical Lutheran Church, rural St. Peter, MN

Jonathan Daniel Aaberg, March 7, 1961, baptized at Naeve Hospital, Albert Lea, MN, by his father, Pastor Theodore A. Aaberg. Affirmation of baptism at Scarville Evangelical Lutheran Church, March 26, 1961. Sponsors: Mr. and Mrs. Clifford Dale, and Mr. and Mrs. Gerhard Olson. Jonathan was confirmed on May 11, 1975, at Norseland Evangelical Lutheran Church, rural St. Peter, MN.

Joel Christian Aaberg, August 1, 1965, baptized at Naeve Hospital, Albert Lea, MN, by his father, Pastor Theodore A. Aaberg. Affirmation of baptism at Scarville Evangelical Lutheran Church, August 15, 1965. Sponsors: Mr. and Mrs. Harry S. Olson, Mr. and Mrs. Lester Storby, and Mrs. Mabel Akre. Joel was confirmed on May 27, 1979, at Mt. Olive Lutheran Church, Mankato, MN.

Grandchildren:

Jennifer Ann Mehlberg, August 7, 1983, baptized at the hospital by her father, Rev. Ronald Mehlberg. Affirmation of baptism at Good Shepherd Lutheran Church, West Bend, WI, on September 18, 1983. Sponsors: Marie Aaberg and Randy Mehlberg.

Shawna Marie Mehlberg, May 9, 1985. baptized at the hospital by her father, Rev. Ronald Mehlberg on May 10, 1985.[1] Affirmation of baptism at Good Shepherd Lutheran Church, West Bend, WI. Sponsors: Shirleen Hahnke and Jonathan Aaberg.

Abby Christina Mehlberg, June 23, 1989, baptized at the hospital by her father, Rev. Ronald Mehlberg. Affirmation of baptism at Good Shepherd Lutheran Church, West Bend, WI, on July 16, 1989. Sponsors: Shirleen Hahnke and Jonathan Aaberg

Clair Nicole Aaberg baptized December 22, 2001, at Norseland Lutheran Church, Rural St. Peter, Minnesota, by Pastor Craig Ferkenstad. Her sponsors were Marie Aaberg and Denise and Melvin Fick.

---

1   Shawna was born only a few minutes before midnight which explains why she was baptized on the 10th of May.

This book is the first trade edition which is substantially the same as the first hand-bound edition with only small corrections generated from the proofreading efforts of Marie Aaberg and notes left by Melvina Aaberg herself. The primary font used is Garamond. The layout was done using Adobe InDesign on a Mac. In order to meet the demand for this edition Two Rooms Press is employing the printing and distribution resources of Lightening Source and Ingram Content Group.